The Medicaid Planning Handbook

The Medicaid Planning Handbook

REVISED AND UPDATED

A Guide to Protecting Your Family's Assets from Catastrophic Nursing Home Costs

Alexander A. Bove, Jr.

LITTLE, BROWN AND COMPANY

Boston   New York   Toronto   London

Second Edition, Revised and Updated

This book is designed to provide accurate information as of the date of
publication. Since federal and state laws change periodically, the book is sold
with the understanding that the publisher is not engaged in rendering legal,
accounting, or other professional service or advice. If legal advice or other
expert assistance is required, the services of a competent professional person
should be sought.

Library of Congress Cataloging-in-Publication Data

Bove, Alexander A.
   The medicaid planning handbook : a guide to protecting your
family's assets from nursing home costs / Alexander A. Bove, Jr. —
2nd ed., rev. and updated.
      p.   cm.
   Includes index.
   ISBN 0-316-10374-8
   1. Medicaid — Law and legislation — Popular works.   2. Estate
planning — United States — Popular works.   3. Aged — Long-term care —
United States — Finance — Planning.   I. Title.
KF3608.A4B68   1996
344.73′022 — dc20
[347.30422]   95-30835

10   9   8   7   6   5   4   3   2

MV-NY

Published simultaneously in Canada
by Little, Brown & Company (Canada) Limited

PRINTED IN THE UNITED STATES OF AMERICA

Contents

CHAPTER FOUR

Strategies to Protect Your Assets

CHAPTER FIVE

Long Term Care Insurance: What to Look for in a Policy

CHAPTER SIX

Durable Power of Attorney: Don't Leave Home Without It!

The Morality of Medicaid Planning: Is It True That "Only the Suckers Pay"?

*A*n article written in late 1989 by a nationally known if not acclaimed financial columnist viciously attacked the practice of Medicaid planning as shameful and "offensive" behavior on the part of the public and advisors alike. The gist of the article was that this type of planning—creating "artificial poverty"—is ultimately paid for by the public. The columnist argued that the Medicaid program is designed to help the "poor" and that it is positively immoral for advisors like me to show readers like you (who presumably are not poor) how to protect your home and life's savings if you or a family member should be faced with the need for expensive long term care.

Our columnist and righteous others who agree with her seem to be totally ignorant of two critical facts: First, the very law which they claim we are abusing tells us clearly that we are expected to pay for nursing home costs only for a specified period of time (generally thirty-six months). After that, the Medicaid law provides that the government will pay, unless we are foolish enough to pass up the opportunity to stop paying. Clearly, arranging assets in a way allowed by the law to qualify for Medicaid is no more immoral than arranging assets to legally qualify for income tax or estate tax savings, (which the columnist herself feels it appropriate to promote on a regular basis).

Second, a truly fair and objective analysis of the *whole* picture would reveal that even in the case of the most aggressive Medicaid plan, it is not the planners who are immoral but the system itself.

Think about it. We have a system that will pay virtually all the medical bills of a *multimillionaire* who has cancer, while stripping a working, middle-class elderly couple of virtually everything they own if one or both have to enter a nursing home. Where is the morality there? And if someone were to show the elderly couple how they could legally protect their home and a little savings, where is the immorality in that? Is it more moral to be a millionaire with cancer than a middle-class old man with Alzheimer's disease?

Use of the argument of morality to denigrate Medicaid planning is without foundation and is put forth only by those few who refuse to address the larger and more important underlying question: How do we as a nation take care of our elderly? And not just the elderly who are "fortunate" enough to be stricken with the right illness (one that will be paid for by the Medicare part of our system).

The Medicaid laws (and those who speak out against Medicaid planning) have overlooked one indisputable fact: a person does not *choose* to develop Alzheimer's disease or multiple sclerosis or paralysis (where costs are *not* paid) over cancer or blood disease or chronic kidney disease (where costs *are* paid). Our health care system has become some sort of morbid lottery whereby the illness you happen to get will determine whether you go bankrupt or not.

In my opinion, it is only a matter of time before these inequities will be recognized and the system will pay for all of us who need care, regardless of our financial situation. In the meantime, however, there are ways to avoid the risk of bankruptcy if you happen to draw the wrong illness, and that's what this book is all about. It covers in great detail all of the available options for protecting assets, including various types of trusts and how to use them, what to do and what *not* to do with your home, and how to protect savings, investments, and retirement-plan funds.

As to the final word on morality, perhaps that must come from within each of us when we are faced with the choice between Medicaid planning or bankruptcy. If, like our friendly columnist, you feel you should pay until virtually everything is gone, you do have that choice. By reading this book, however, at least you will be aware of your other options.

Alexander A. Bove, Jr.

The Medicaid Planning Handbook

CHAPTER ONE

The Way It Is

*I*n the beginning there was the Green family and the Benson family. Herb Green and Rob Benson knew each other well, as they had worked almost side by side for the same company for nearly thirty years. Both families consisted of a husband and wife in their late sixties and two adult children. Both families had their own homes and a comfortable amount of savings. And coincidentally, both families were stricken with catastrophic illness at about the same time.

There was one major difference, however. Herb's illness, costly as it was, was covered by insurance and did not affect the financial security of his family, while Rob's illness, which in fact was less costly to treat than Herb's, left Rob's family nearly bankrupt. Here are their stories.

Herb Green worked most of his life at Boston Edison and retired at age sixty-five. After the children left for college, Herb's wife, Mary, resumed her teaching position with the city of Medford, just outside Boston, and worked there until she retired, also at sixty-five. Subsequently, a routine physical disclosed that Herb had prostate cancer that was at an advanced stage. Herb's doctor prescribed extensive tests and then chemotherapy and radiation treatments. Ultimately, surgery was required, as well as extensive follow-up treatment that included home visits by nurses. Treatment would continue for the rest of Herb's life, with costs running in the hundreds of thousands of dollars, virtually all to be paid by the Medicare program together with the Greens' supplemental health insurance coverage. As a result, the Greens retained the security of their home and just about every penny of their savings.

Rob Benson also retired at sixty-five, but his wife, Betty, continued to work past that age, intending to retire later with extra benefits. Shortly after Rob's retirement, Betty began noticing that Rob was becoming increasingly forgetful. At first it was almost humorous and cute, but as the condition worsened, Betty became frightened and fearful, not only for Rob's safety but also for her own security. She took Rob to specialists for several tests and he was finally diagnosed as having Alzheimer's disease. The doctor told Betty there was no meaningful treatment and that she must simply keep an eye on him and care for him at home as long as she could.

Betty took care of Rob for about a year (she had to retire from her job before she had planned to), but eventually the task was more than she could handle. Even the part-time nurses she hired to care for Rob at home were not enough. He needed constant care and supervision. Finally, she resigned herself to the fact that Rob would have to enter a nursing home.

When Rob was admitted to the nursing home, Betty was required to complete forms that disclosed every detail of their financial situation, including savings, investments, life insurance, retirement income, and so on, not only for the nursing home but also for their state's Department of Public Welfare, which administers the Medicaid program. Shortly after Betty completed these forms, the department sent a notice to Betty advising her that all of Rob's pension income would have to be spent on his care. In addition, Betty would have to spend all but about $75,000 of their savings toward Rob's care before she could expect any help from the state and federal government. That is, she would be allowed to keep about $75,000 from their joint savings so that she wouldn't be "impoverished." This amount, she was told, was to provide her with financial security!

It didn't take Betty long to figure that at a cost of about $50,000 per year for Rob's nursing home, in about three years she would have spent about $150,000 of their savings on Rob's care and would then be down to the required $75,000 she was "allowed" to keep. "But then," Betty thought, "what if *I* get sick?" And Betty's concern was well placed. If she should get sick, as her husband did, then there would go not only the rest of the family's money but probably their home as well.*

Such is the state of our system and a stark illustration of the difference between *Medicare* (the Green family case) and *Medicaid* (the Benson family case). Those lucky enough to be stricken with the right type of illness can retain their financial security; the others will be forced into bankruptcy. There are, however, steps that can legally be taken to protect a family's financial security in the face of a long term illness.

In fact, in many respects the Medicaid laws are like the tax laws — you can get the advice of experts and take maximum legal advantage of the laws and pay much less, or you can ignore them or fail to get proper advice and pay much more. The critical difference, however, between the tax laws and the Medicaid laws is that ignorance of the Medicaid laws can cost you everything you own. Therefore, you should first understand the primary difference between Medicare and Medicaid.

Medicaid versus Medicare

The difference of two letters in Medica__re__ and Medica__id__ can spell bankruptcy!

---

* For convenience and in order to be consistent with statistics, in this book all the examples and case studies dealing with a married couple show the husband as the spouse who enters a nursing home. No inferences should be drawn from this.

Because the terms Medicare and Medicaid are so similar, most people confuse the two. But, as we have seen in the comparison of the Greens and the Bensons, the difference can be crucial. Briefly, the Medicare program covers *medical* needs, as in Herb Green's case, as opposed to *custodial* care, as in the case of Rob Benson. Medicare is *not* a financially need based program, and, therefore, the Medicare program pays for all necessary medical treatment *regardless* of the recipient's financial status (that is, you can be quite rich and still qualify for Medicare).

Although Medicare does not pay for nursing home costs, the federal Medicare Catastrophic Coverage Act (commonly referred to as "MECCA"), enacted in 1988, adds to the confusion, since it allows Medicare to pay up to *100* days of nursing home costs that previously were, for the most part, paid by *Medicaid* only for patients who qualified for welfare benefits, since such long term care costs were not deemed to be medically necessary. In fact, even now, Medicare may pay these costs only if the nursing home care is medically necessary, but will not pay for intermediate or custodial care (such as that required for an Alzheimer's patient). And since the average nursing home stay is thirty months or more, it is the *Medicaid* program that more often provides the costs of long term care, but *only if* the patient is eligible for benefits (that is, considered *needy*).

Unlike the Medicare program, the Medicaid program is *need based,* providing benefits only to those patients who demonstrate a financial need, which is determined by federal guidelines modified to a certain extent by the state. In other words, since benefits are based on financial *need,* or your inability to pay for yourself, *you cannot have more than a limited amount of cash or other available assets. If you do, you'll be required to use it for your care before the state will pay!*

To Illustrate

Frank, age seventy, lives with his mother in her home. His only assets consist of a savings account of $18,000, which he uses not only for himself but also to help his mother. Frank suffers a stroke and soon after must be admitted to a nursing home. Before he can qualify for Medicaid, Frank must spend all but about $2,000* of his assets. Despite the fact that Frank's aged mother may be dependent on him, she is not entitled to keep his money.

The Medicaid program is implemented by each state individually. The federal government is involved because it reimburses the state for a substantial portion of Medicaid benefits paid to its citizens, provided the state's Medicaid program meets the prescribed federal guidelines. Hence, the states tend to follow the dictates of the federal government, and their Medicaid laws are substantially similar.

Even though the program is need based, however, I will show you how a family can restructure its assets so as to qualify for Medicaid benefits, while preserving at least some of its assets for the remaining healthy members of the family. To do this, one must first understand how an individual's assets are regarded ("counted") for Medicaid purposes.

Who Can Qualify for Medicaid?

Helen, age fifty-six, lives with her thirty-year-old daughter, Jean, in Helen's home. Helen has multiple sclerosis. Up to now, Jean has been able to care for her, but the disease has progressed to a point where Helen will have to be institutionalized soon. Because of the high costs involved, both Helen and Jean are concerned about whether they can get any help in paying for these costs. Basically, all Helen has is her home, and she doesn't want to lose it. Her only income is Social Security. Will she qualify for Medicaid?

To be eligible to receive Medicaid benefits, a person must meet three eligibility tests: eligibility based on *category* (age or disability); eligibility based on *income;* and eligibility based on *assets.*

---

* There is a maximum amount that an individual may retain. It varies from state to state, ranging from $999 to $4,000.

Eligibility Based on Age or Disability

First, the individual must be in need of nursing home or custodial care *and* must fall into one of the categories eligible for benefits (called "categorical" eligibility). The individual must be either age sixty-five or older, or blind, or physically or mentally disabled. In other words, a forty-five-year-old blind or disabled person could qualify for nursing home benefits, provided he meets the other two tests I will discuss. On the other hand, a sixty-six-year-old need not be disabled in any way except that he must need long term care, and he must also meet the two tests later described.

In Helen's case, therefore, it appears that since she has multiple sclerosis, she can qualify for Medicaid because of her disability, *provided* she meets the other two tests.

Eligibility Based on Income

Under this test, the individual may not have monthly income in excess of the allowable amount set by the state. This amount is adjusted from time to time and varies from state to state. If a person had income from *any* source, *whether taxable or not,* in excess of the allowable limit, he would not qualify for Medicaid. However, most states are "spend-down" states, meaning that if the person were to *spend* his income (less a small personal allowance) on nursing home costs, he would then be able to receive Medicaid benefits for the balance of his long term care costs.

Therefore, if Helen's income is less than the allowable amount for Medicaid purposes, she will qualify for benefits under this test. If it exceeds the allowable amount and she lives in a "spend-down" state, she may still be eligible, provided she spends her income toward her nursing home care.

To Illustrate

Say that Helen's income is $850 per month from Social Security. She enters a nursing home, and the monthly nursing home costs are $3,600. She applies for Medicaid. The state Helen lives in provides that the maximum allowable income is $650 per month. Although Helen's income of $850 exceeds the allowable amount, which, by itself, would disqualify her from receiving benefits, if she "spends down" her income on her long-term care costs, then Medicaid will pay the balance of the nursing home costs. In this case, therefore, if Helen spends the $850 per month (less a small personal needs allowance) on her care, Medicaid will pay the balance of the costs for her care.

Important Note _____

Some states, for example, Florida, New Jersey, and Tennessee, are *"income cap"* states, which *do not* allow a spend-down of income. (For a complete list, see Appendix A). In these states, if the individual has income that exceeds the limit by even one dollar, she cannot qualify for Medicaid regardless of her condition or need for care, and regardless of the extent of any other assets she has. (But see Chapter 4 on one way to deal with this in extreme cases.)

For an unmarried individual in an income cap state who receives an income just over the cap, this can spell disaster, particularly if the person has few or no other assets. In some cases, it may be possible for the individual to correct this problem by disclaiming or rejecting the excess income. Unfortunately, it is not always possible to do this, as in the case of Social Security payments or pension income.

Tip _____

To help deal with this dilemma, the 1993 change in the Medicaid law now allows the Medicaid applicant, or someone on his or her behalf, to submit legal petitions to establish a trust that limits the person's income *by court order* to an amount one dollar *below* the income cap, thereby qualifying the person to receive Medicaid benefits in that state. For specific rules that must be followed, see Chapter 4.

Where a married couple is concerned, once a spouse is in a nursing home, each spouse's income is considered separately (even in income cap states), so that the healthy spouse will be allowed to keep all of her own income. The obvious problem occurs, however, where the bulk or all of the income is being received by the institutionalized spouse.

Important Note

> For Medicaid purposes, after the first month of institutionalization, there is no requirement that the healthy spouse pay for the care of the institutionalized spouse. But what about the healthy spouse's right to the income of the institutionalized spouse?

The 1989 federal Medicaid rules (MECCA) have somewhat modified the income rules, to favor, surprisingly, the *healthy* spouse, provided she does not have too much income of her own. Each spouse is still entitled to keep his or her own income, but if the income of the healthy spouse is below the amount determined by the state to be the "minimum monthly maintenance needs allowance" as prescribed by the Medicaid rules (in this book I call it the "spousal income allowance"), then she will be granted an amount from the income of the institutionalized spouse (assuming he has income) sufficient to bring her income up to the spousal income allowance granted to her.

The spousal income allowance is based on a somewhat complicated formula tied to multiples of the federal poverty level standards and an "excess shelter allowance." The latter means that the state must consider the shelter costs of the healthy spouse, including rent, mortgage, or maintenance payments, plus utilities. In my opinion, it is not necessary that you be able to mathematically compute the formula, since it will be computed for you by the state.

To Illustrate

> Say that John has been admitted to a nursing home and his wife, Mary, remains at home. John's income from a pension and Social Security is $2,300 per month. Mary's income is only $600 per month. Upon Mary's request, the state determines that Mary's spousal income allowance is $1,500 per month. Mary then would be allowed to receive from John's income the difference between the $1,500 allowance and the amount of

her own income (that is, $1,500 less $600), or $900 from John's monthly income. The balance of John's income ($2,300 less $900, or $1,400 per month) would be applied toward his nursing home care.

Note _____

If John and Mary lived in an income cap state, then John's remaining income of $1,400 per month could not exceed the allowable cap. If it did, he would not qualify for Medicaid.

Important Notes _____

• In determining which spouse is entitled to the income, the Medicaid rules apply the "name-on-the-check" rule. That is, if the income is paid to John, as under a company pension or IRA, then it is *his* income. If the income is paid to John and Mary together, as in dividends or interest paid from a joint account or from a trust where no division or share is indicated, the income is considered to belong one-half to each of them.

If income is payable to Mary, because the savings or investments are in her name or because the terms of a trust direct the trustee to pay income to Mary, then it is considered *Mary's* income and will not be available to pay for John's care.

• The spousal income allowance is not normally established by the state until the institutionalized spouse applies for Medicaid. Since this may not occur until months or even years after the spouse is institutionalized, waiting until that time to plan can cause the family to lose important opportunities to save assets. However, the institutionalized spouse or the healthy spouse (or a representative of either) at any time after a spouse is institutionalized, may *request* that the state establish the healthy spouse's income allowance, and it is usually a good idea to do so (after you have consulted an expert). (See further discussion of this in Chapter 4, "Strategies to Protect Your Assets.")

• The maximum spousal income allowance under the Medicaid rules is $1,500 per month*, but this may be increased if the

_____
* For 1995, this amount was increased to $1,870 per month in accordance with the inflationary index.

healthy spouse can convince the state that she actually needs more, owing to exceptional circumstances. Also, the law allows the maximum to be adjusted for inflation over the years. Finally, since a couple's income is usually dependent to a great extent on the income from their investments and savings, the amount of assets the healthy spouse is allowed to keep may vary, depending upon the income produced by such assets. For this reason (as explained later in greater detail), a clear understanding of the "assets test" is very important.

• Remember, Medicaid counts all types of income, from whatever source. It does not matter whether it is taxable or not.

The Assets Test: How Much (and What) You Can Keep

The third test that must be met limits the total amount of assets (sometimes called "resources") a person may have before he can qualify for Medicaid benefits. Under this test there are two basic categories of assets: *countable assets,* the total value of which will determine a person's eligibility for Medicaid, and *noncountable* (or "exempt") *assets,* which, regardless of value (except in certain cases), will *not* affect a person's eligibility. A hybrid category is called *inaccessible assets.* These are assets which by themselves may be countable (such as cash or securities) but are held under such circumstances that they are considered "inaccessible" to the applicant (such as assets held in certain irrevocable trusts — discussed later).

Basically, all assets (everything you own) are countable except those that are expressly exempt *under the law or those that are considered inaccessible to the individual.*

To be eligible to receive Medicaid benefits, generally a person may not have more than $2,000 of countable assets*, and a married couple (but only if living together), not more than $3,000 of countable assets. Since it is relatively rare for a couple living together to apply for and qualify for Medicaid, and since spouses are treated as individuals one month after either of them enters a nursing home,

---

* This figure ranges from $999 to $4,000, but in the majority of states it is $2,000.

this discussion will deal only with the requirement of an *individual,* even though he or she may be married.

Following are assets which you can own which will *not* affect your eligibility to receive Medicaid benefits (these are called non-countable assets):

1. Your home (principal residence), regardless of value.

2. Household belongings, furnishings, personal effects, and jewelry (some states limit the value of these items).

3. A burial account of up to $1,500 in most states, higher in some. (Note: This is different from a burial *contract.*)

4. Burial plots for the individual or members of the family.

5. Prepaid noncancelable burial contracts.

6. Cash value of life insurance policies, provided the face value does not exceed $1,500.

7. Term life insurance policies (with no cash value) up to any amount in face value.

8. One automobile for use by the individual and his family.

9. Inaccessible assets of any value.

10. Company pension funds and certain Keogh funds.

11. Certain trust funds.

12. In addition, most states allow a person to retain certain income-producing property that is "essential to their self-support."

1. The principal residence. This is normally the largest non-countable asset a family will have, and it is quite a "gift" that the government treats it as exempt, regardless of its value. However, since the exemption is technically limited to the home (and the accompanying land) "*used* as the principal place of residence," questions arise when, for instance, the residence ceases to be a residence because the owner is in a nursing home and it is uncertain he will ever return, or when the Medicaid applicant owns and lives in a two- or three-family residence. Is the entire residence noncountable or only the one-half (or one-third) used by the applicant and his family? And what about any rents that he receives from the other units?

Federal regulations provide that only the portion occupied as a principal residence is exempt, indicating that our owner-occupied multiple-family dwelling would be only partially exempt. To date, however, particularly if the applicant leaves "family" in the home, it has been the policy of the Medicaid authorities to treat the entire residence as exempt, even though it may be a two- or three-family home. If the other apartments are rented, however, Medicaid authorities will definitely require that "excess" rents (over allowable expenses in carrying the property) be applied to pay nursing home costs.

This practice is not, of course, without reasonable limits and varies from state to state. No doubt if the applicant owned and lived in a twelve-unit apartment house, the policy would not be the same, so don't count on it.

Important Note

> If the multifamily residence *is* treated as the applicant's residence by the state, then it should follow that it would be treated as such for all purposes, including transfers to other family members as discussed in Chapter 4.

Tip

> Though in most states the home is noncountable during the lifetime of the applicant, the state is likely to try to place a lien on it during the individual's lifetime, and in any event they will come after it on the death of the institutionalized person. See Chapter 8 for a discussion of liens and estate recovery.

Important Note

> The home is not treated the same way in all states. Be sure to check with a local expert to determine your state's rules.

2. Household belongings, etc. Some states limit the noncountable value of these items. But generally, no inventory is taken, and despite the occasional inequity in which, for instance, one family has countable cash while another has several thousands of dollars worth of noncountable oriental rugs, the rule can operate to protect substantial assets in some cases.

Tip

> *Do not* rush out and buy oriental rugs, paintings, or the like, as this could be disastrous from a Medicaid standpoint. As a general rule, only the purchase of reasonable and necessary household or personal items should be considered. If you already have such items and have had them for years, it is likely they can be retained in the family.

3. Segregated burial account. This can simply be a bank account of up to $1,500 (more in some states), created by the applicant or anyone else on his behalf (presumably with his funds) and labeled "John Smith, burial account" or "John Smith, for burial purposes only." It can be controllable by John and/or his wife or anyone else who is assigned to use the funds for this purpose. However, the funds should *not* be withdrawn prior to death (unless applied to burial or funeral expenses), nor used for any other purpose. If there happens to be any unused balance after payment of funeral and burial expenses, it is supposed to be paid over to the state.

4. Burial plots for the individual and his family. These may be of any value and may be purchased at any time. The plots need not be located in the individual's home state, though they must be verifiable burial plots. A spot marked off in the yard of your beach-front cottage is not likely to qualify.

5. Prepaid, noncancelable burial contracts. In the case of an elderly person who is ill and permanently institutionalized, purchasing such a contract often makes a good deal of sense. If you are reasonably certain as to where the funeral and burial will take place, you can enter into a contract with the funeral home and make payment in full without affecting the individual's Medicaid eligibility. This is usually done in the form of an irrevocable burial trust. This is a "form" trust offered by the funeral parlor or the state. Once funded, the trust funds may not be used for any other purpose, and any excess funds remaining in the trust after the person is buried are supposed to be made available to the Department of Public Welfare to repay Medicaid benefits. The trustee of this trust is usually the funeral home itself. Be sure to provide that a successor trustee (a funeral home) may be chosen by a member of the family if the first choice is unable to perform under the trust agreement (as in the case of bankruptcy or dissolution of the first funeral home).

Tip

Be sure to select a funeral home that has an unimpeachable reputation and a strong financial condition — ask for references. And be sure the contract you sign spells out all the details of the funeral.

6. Cash value of life insurance contracts of up to $1,500 face value. The face value of a policy is the amount that the insurance company will pay when the insured dies. If the total *face value* of all life insurance contracts (policies) owned by the applicant exceeds $1,500, then the total *cash value* of such policies becomes countable. However, if such policies (whether on the life of the applicant or on someone else's life) are owned by someone other than the applicant or the applicant's spouse and if the applicant did not transfer the policies within the disqualifying thirty-six-month waiting period discussed later, then the cash value of the policies will not be countable.

Note

Do not confuse ownership of a policy with designation of a beneficiary. They are not the same. If you want to transfer ownership of a policy, you must sign an "irrevocable assignment form." It is the owner of the policy who has the right to name the beneficiary or to cash in the policy.

Tip

If the cash value of the policies *does* exceed $1,500 (total for *all* of the policies owned by the applicant and/or his spouse), check the policy to see just how much insurance you really have — for example, a $5,000 policy with $3,200 of cash value may only be $1,800 of life insurance. In a case like this, consider exchanging the policy for a *joint and survivor annuity* (a contract that makes periodic payments until the death of the surviving spouse), or simply an annuity for the *healthy* spouse, if applicable. This would only work between *spouses*. Otherwise, the annuity will be countable. (For more on this, see Chapter 4.)

7. Term life insurance policies up to any amount of face value. Since term life insurance policies have no cash value, there is nothing to count, regardless of the face value of the policy (the amount the insurance company will pay on the applicant's death). If the policy *does* have cash value, then the rule discussed in item 6 will apply.

Tip _____

Be sure to recheck the beneficiary designation on these policies. The beneficiary *should not* be the estate of the insured, since this would cause the proceeds to pass through the deceased's probate estate, subjecting the proceeds to claims (including Medicaid liens), probate fees, and additional expenses. It may be all right for the spouse to be the beneficiary, provided the spouse is in good health and unlikely to enter a nursing home. And if the policy is payable to the spouse, be sure that a "contingent" beneficiary is named, in case the spouse predeceases the institutionalized person.

8. One automobile for use by the individual and his family. If the applicant owns more than one automobile, he may choose the one that he wants to be exempt (obviously he would choose the most expensive one). Some states place a limit, such as $4,500, on the exempt value of an auto, but in many states there is no limit to the value of the exempt auto. In the no-limit states, technically, you could use the applicant's $180,000 of countable assets to purchase a Rolls-Royce Corniche convertible (though I *don't* recommend it), and he would then immediately qualify for Medicaid. Finally, note that the applicant can own an exempt auto even though he does not or cannot drive, so long as the auto is used primarily for family transportation purposes (chopped motorcycles and recreational vehicles generally do not qualify).

Tip _____

> Whether it is a Rolls-Royce or a Toyota, don't rush out and buy a car unless there is some reasonable need for doing so. Some states are attacking such purchases by arguing that the auto was bought solely for the purpose of qualifying for Medicaid. You are particularly vulnerable to this attack where there is no apparent need for the applicant or his family to have a new car. I have seen several Medicaid applications denied because the applicant, without good cause, purchased a car just before applying for benefits. And most of these cases are lost on appeal, leaving the family with no Medicaid benefits until it sells the car (usually at a loss) and spends the proceeds down to the allowable amount.

9. Inaccessible assets of any value. An inaccessible asset is "an asset to which the individual has no ready access either directly or through legal proceedings," according to most state regulations. However, if the individual gains access at some future date, the asset will then become countable. An asset is accessible if at any time the applicant has a legal share of it *and* the right to use or liquidate that share. Therefore, if an individual is going to rely on an asset being inaccessible, it should generally be *permanently* inaccessible to the individual, but at the same time, it should be accessible to someone else. Otherwise it is of no use to the family.

10. Company pension funds and certain Keogh funds. Funds in a pension plan created by your employer are generally not counted until accessible to you, such as upon reaching retirement age or permanent disability. Funds in an IRA (Individual Retirement Account) or Keogh account are generally considered fully accessible, less any penalties the applicant would pay on withdrawal. One exception to this is a situation in which the applicant (who was self-employed) set up a Keogh plan but covered *other* employees in the plan besides himself and his family. In this case, his Keogh funds are considered inaccessible.

Tip _____

> If funds are already withdrawn from an IRA or Keogh (or from a pension plan of any sort) and the state attempts to count them in full, you should immediately determine (as closely as possible) the federal and state tax due on account of the withdrawal and pay it without delay. Payment of the tax (and any applicable penalties) is a transfer for valid consideration (reduction of the tax liability), and therefore, it will *not* trigger a period of disqualification. If you do not pay the tax, you'll still owe it and the state will still count the full amount of the withdrawn retirement-plan funds. If the funds are still in the plan, however, see Case Study 8 (in Chapter 11) for a possible strategy.

11. Certain trust funds. Until late 1993, the most useful application of the concept of inaccessibility (see item 9), from the standpoint of protection of assets, was through the use of certain *trusts*. Although discussed later in much greater detail, the general rule is that for purposes of Medicaid eligibility, the state can count only those assets that the trustees can legally pay out or distribute to the applicant under the terms of the trust, and this is *still* the case. However, as we will see, the government has lengthened the waiting period, making the planning with trusts a little more difficult.

To Illustrate _____

> John transfers all of his savings to a trust which provides that he and his wife, Mary, are to receive all of the income and none of the principal for their lives. Neither one has any powers to change or terminate the trust. In this case, after the prescribed waiting period, the trust principal will be *inaccessible* to both spouses and therefore *not* countable for Medicaid purposes. (See more on trusts in Chapter 4.)

Only *irrevocable* (unchangeable) trusts can protect otherwise countable assets, such as cash or securities, for Medicaid purposes. This means that once such a trust is done and funded with your assets, you may be stuck with it, so be sure you get a *second opinion* on your plan before you sign on the dotted line. (See more on this in Chapter 4.)

12. Income-producing property "essential to self-support." Generally, this category includes assets that are not readily reducible to cash and that are producing steady income that is essential to the support of the individual and his family. A typical example might be the case of an individual who owns a small business that is producing the primary source of income for himself and his spouse. Although the business is technically an asset that could be liquidated, liquidation would not be easy and it would cut off the very income that is supporting the individual and his spouse. In such a case, the state will normally treat the asset (here, the small business) as exempt, so long as it is not sold and continues to produce income to contribute to the support of the individual and/or his spouse. Some states place a limit on the length of time they will allow this asset to continue to be exempt. Check the law in your particular state before relying on the exemption.

Jointly Held Assets

Medicaid rules distinguish joint bank accounts from all other jointly held assets. Joint bank accounts are presumed to be owned entirely by the Medicaid applicant unless the (healthy) joint owner (or owners) other than the spouse can prove to the satisfaction of the authorities that a specific portion of the accounts was contributed by her.

Where husband and wife are the only joint owners, a showing of contribution is unimportant because the Medicaid rules now count the assets of *both* spouses when one is institutionalized.

In those cases where someone *other than* a spouse is a joint owner, the healthy joint owner should be able to show that she has made identifiable contributions to the account or offer other acceptable "proof" of her share. If this cannot be shown, then the entire amount in the joint bank account will be treated as belonging to the applicant for Medicaid purposes and it must be spent toward nursing home costs (or applied in some other acceptable way) before Medicaid benefits will be paid. Conversely, if the other (nonspouse) joint owner can show contributions, then the portion contributed will not be regarded as part of the applicant's assets.

In addition to the treatment as countable assets, jointly held assets (or assets held as tenants in common) with the applicant can give rise to another problem. If the applicant's actual ownership share of the jointly held asset is reduced (whether by withdrawal or any other way), the amount of the reduction will be treated as a transfer by the applicant and could result in a disqualification from benefits for a period of time. (See Chapter 3 for further details.)

Tip

If someone other than a spouse did contribute to the account, start now gathering whatever proof you can of such contributions stemming from the other joint owner — that is, deposit receipts with notes written on them, showing that deposit amounts are exactly equal to a paycheck stub or inheritance, and so on.

Fortunately, in cases where there is no documentation available, Medicaid regulations generally allow a joint owner to submit an affidavit (sworn statement) as support for her contributions to the joint account, showing where her share of the funds came from. The probability of success of such an affidavit is difficult to predict, but one should certainly be submitted if other documentation is lost or unavailable.

All other jointly held assets, including real estate, stocks or other securities, promissory notes, and money market accounts, are treated as if each joint owner owned an equal share of the account, regardless of contribution. It is possible, however, for the healthy joint owner to refute this presumption of equal ownership when the healthy joint owner can prove that more than half the joint assets were hers or attributable to her contributions.

Important Note _____

> In some cases, more than half of the jointly held assets will be counted, *despite* this rule. To illustrate, say that Dad has $80,000 in a bank account. He withdraws these funds and purchases $80,000 worth of Terminal Motors stock in joint names with his son. If Dad applies for Medicaid within the thirty-six-month waiting period (after the purchase), the state is very likely to count the entire $80,000 value of the stock as Dad's funds, despite the equal presumption rule. (See more on this in Chapter 4.)

Tip _____

> As a general rule, jointly held assets spell trouble. Therefore, as a second general rule, *stay out of joint!*

Some of these details may seem technical to you, but you must keep in mind that protection of your assets requires at least a general understanding of the rules. This must begin with an understanding of what assets are at risk — hence I have described above the basic rules of "countable" assets. From here we will learn how these rules of countability can change if you are married, and from there, what you can do, whether married or single, to take advantage of the rules, so that you will not have to worry that what happened to the Benson family will happen to you, and so that you and your family can avoid bankruptcy if long term illness strikes.

CHAPTER TWO

Married — to Be or Not to Be? That Is the Medicaid Question!

*A*lthough Helen realized she would ultimately have to place her husband, Fred, in a nursing home, when it actually happened she was devastated. Helen felt a terrible, painful loneliness and a deep sense of shame for having deserted her husband of over forty years. But the worst was yet to come.

When Fred entered the nursing home, Helen was advised by the home that she would have to complete a financial questionnaire showing all of their assets (both Fred's *and* Helen's) so that their state's Medicaid people could tell Helen just how much she could keep and how much she would have to spend on Fred's care before he might qualify for Medicaid to pay his nursing home costs (which were about $5,000 per month). This "snapshot" of the family finance was required, Helen was told, even though Fred might not apply for Medicaid until months or even years from then.

Helen completed the form, which disclosed that the couple had a home in joint names, savings of about $42,000, also in joint names, an automobile, and about $124,000 in stock in Helen's name that Helen had inherited from her parents. The only other asset was Helen's IRA, which contained about $11,500. To Helen's surprise, the form did not ask about any mortgage or other debts that they owed.

After Helen completed the form, she sent it along to the Medicaid authorities, and a short while later, they told Helen that before Fred could qualify for Medicaid, she would have to spend about $100,000 toward Fred's care. Helen could keep only $74,820 for her own "needs"!

"But this is my money," Helen argued in desperation. "It belonged to my parents and Fred had nothing to do with it. If I spend that, I'll have nothing for myself!" So goes the new Medicaid law called MECCA and the "pooling of assets" rule for spouses.

It was not always "what's mine is yours." Before MECCA, each spouse could keep his or her individual assets without affecting the eligibility of the other to receive Medicaid benefits. However, if it was the wealthy spouse who entered a nursing home, the "poor" spouse at home would quickly become poorer, perhaps to the point of near poverty. Intending to prevent this, Congress enacted the portion of MECCA sometimes referred to as the Spousal Impoverishment Act. In theory, at least, the act is intended to allow the healthy spouse to keep a certain amount of the ill spouse's assets and not go "bankrupt." Unfortunately, as seen in Helen's case above, the same rule can have a devastating effect if it is the poor spouse who enters a nursing home. In either event, here is how the pooling of assets rule works.*

For a spouse who was institutionalized *on or after September 30, 1989,* MECCA calls for a determination of *all countable assets of both spouses* to be taken at the time of institutionalization, so that a "spousal resource allowance" can be established for the "at home" (healthy) spouse. Assets in excess of this spousal resource allowance are then counted for purposes of determining whether the institutionalized spouse will qualify for Medicaid. Note that, as illustrated

---

* These rules apply only where the institutionalized person has a spouse. As discussed later, the rules for single or divorced persons are totally different.

above, *it does not matter that the healthy spouse owned all the assets or where the assets originally came from. All assets, owned by or available to either spouse, however held, are pooled for this purpose.*

Important Notes

• The spousal *resource* allowance is separate and distinct from the spousal *income* allowance, but as discussed in Chapter 4, increasing the income allowance can in some cases increase the resource allowance.

• After the pooling, a spousal resource allowance equal to one-half the total countable assets is allowed for the healthy spouse, but the allowance can be no more than $60,000* and no less than $12,000.* (A state can elect to increase the minimum, so that the healthy spouse might be able to keep more in cases of small estates. In fact, California, Hawaii, Mississippi, Kentucky, New York, Washington, and Wisconsin have all set their minimum at $60,000.*) The following chart illustrates how the minimum and maximum allowance work:

Countable Assets of Both Spouses	If State's *Min.* Allowance Is	If State's *Max.* Allowance Is	The Healthy Spouse Can Keep
$15,000	$12,000*	$60,000	12,000*
20,000	12,000	60,000	12,000
50,000	12,000	60,000	25,000
70,000	12,000	60,000	35,000
70,000	60,000*	60,000	60,000*
100,000	60,000	60,000	60,000
150,000	60,000	60,000	60,000
200,000	60,000	60,000	60,000

• The financial snapshot is not taken automatically by the state. To have it done at the time of institutionalization, a

* For 1995, these amounts have been increased to $74,820 and $14,964, respectively, in accordance with the inflationary index.

spouse must request it, and, believe it or not, the state may charge a fee for taking it (although states now compute the spousal allowance free of charge). If no request is made, then it may be that no determination of the spousal allowance is made by the state until an application is made for Medicaid benefits, which could be many months after institutionalization. (For determinations made at this time, no fee may be charged.)

• At the time of Medicaid application, even though this may occur long after the date of admission to the nursing home, the state will undertake to determine what the total spousal assets were *at the time of institutionalization.* For this reason, spouses should be careful to document their assets at all times, and *particularly* at the time of institutionalization.

Tips

• Since the snapshot of assets taken to determine the spousal resource allowance must be determined as of the time of institutionalization, even though the application for Medicaid benefits may occur later, *it may be important in some cases to plan BEFORE a spouse is institutionalized,* if possible.

• In any event, if a spouse disagrees with the amount of the spousal resource allowance granted by the state, she may appeal this decision by requesting a "fair hearing" (at the time of application for Medicaid), as discussed in Chapter 9, to seek an increase in her spousal resource allowance on the basis that the amount allowed by the state will not adequately provide for her needs.

• Another exception to the rule can come about if the healthy spouse obtains a court order directing the institutionalized spouse to transfer assets or income to her.

• After the spousal resource allowance is determined by the state (or by a court order), the applicant (or institutionalized spouse) *must* transfer assets representing the designated allowance to the healthy spouse, usually within ninety days of the state's determination of eligibility for Medicaid. Under certain circumstances (where a guardianship or conservatorship is required, for instance), the ninety-day period may be extended by the state.

• If an amount equal to the spousal resource allowance is not transferred to the healthy spouse within the required period, she could *lose* the allowance, since those assets left available to the institutionalized spouse after the required period would then be fully countable.

• Once the spousal resource allowance is determined and the institutionalized spouse becomes eligible for Medicaid, then, as of the beginning of the month following the month in which he is determined eligible for benefits, *the healthy spouse can freely receive or acquire assets of any value without affecting the institutionalized spouse's benefits.* That is, the spousal resource allowance is only determined *once* during any period of continuous institutionalization. Therefore, unless there is a break in the period (as discussed later), the snapshot will not be taken again, even if the healthy spouse later strikes it rich.

To Illustrate

Say that John enters a nursing home in February of 1995, and his wife, Mary, is allowed $50,000 (one-half of their countable assets of $100,000) as her spousal resource allowance. Seven months later, on September 10, John is determined to be eligible for Medicaid, and Mary still has her $50,000 allowance. On November 1, Mary inherits $200,000 from the estate of her deceased sister, increasing Mary's total assets to $250,000. This will have *no* effect on John's Medicaid benefits, and Mary can keep all of these funds.

• Finally, a critical question in the determination of the spousal resource allowance is: what is the "beginning of a continuous period of institutionalization"? This is important because it is the date on which the asset snapshot is taken and, therefore, can determine the financial security of the healthy spouse. The law in most states provides that a continuous period is one in which the institutionalized spouse is expected to remain (and does remain) institutionalized for more than thirty days. Correspondingly, if an institutionalized spouse *leaves* the institution for a period of at least thirty days (and does not apply for Medicaid during that period), this is considered a break in institutionalization and any snapshot taken before that is disregarded. A *new* snapshot must be taken on the date of a subsequent period of "continuous" institutionalization to determine the spousal resource allowance.

To Illustrate

If a spouse has already been institutionalized for more than thirty days and a new snapshot is desired for purposes of protecting assets, it is possible in some (but certainly not all) cases to *remove* the spouse from the institution and care for him at home for an interim period of at least thirty days. This will provide a new opportunity to plan during that period, and when the spouse reenters the nursing home, a *new* snapshot will be taken.

Note

• It is also important to understand that the term "institutionalization," for these purposes, includes entrance into a *hospital,* as well as a nursing home. This is significant because many individuals enter a nursing home directly from or shortly after a hospital stay. In such cases, unless there is a break of at least thirty days between the two, the period of institutionalization for Medicaid purposes begins with the patient's entrance into the hospital rather than the nursing home.

• There are many other special issues relating to Medicaid planning for married couples, including antenuptial or premarital agreements where second marriages are concerned (discussed in Chapter 4) and transfers of assets between spouses (discussed in Chapters 3 and 4).

Can You Protect Assets by Giving Them Away?

The Transfer of Assets Rule

Bill lived with his only child, Alice, who had been helping take care of Bill since his wife died about eight years ago. Because of his increasing incapacity due to a stroke, it was clear that Bill would have to enter a nursing home before the year was out. All Bill had was a small pension and about $75,000 in savings, and, since Alice was not well off, Bill wanted to preserve what little he had for her. Therefore, rather than wait until he entered a nursing home, Bill decided to turn over his $75,000 savings to Alice immediately. A few months later, Alice could no longer care for Bill at home, and he had to be placed in a nursing home.

Shortly after he was admitted to the home, Bill applied for Medicaid since he had no assets. When the Medicaid people reviewed copies of Bill's bank statements (in just about every case, the Medicaid authorities will review bank and other financial statements covering a period of up to thirty-six months prior to the Medicaid application), they discovered that Bill had made a gift of all his savings to Alice. In view of this, Bill's application for Medicaid benefits was denied. As far as the authorities were concerned, Bill "had" $75,000 of assets, and he would not qualify for Medicaid benefits until he spent this down to $2,000.

The Medicaid program is *need based,* providing benefits to those who do not have the finances to provide for themselves. If it were simply a matter of giving away all your funds to qualify for Medicaid just before entering a nursing home (and thereby establishing a *need*), everyone would do it. To discourage people from making such gifts to family members and others and then applying for Medicaid benefits, the laws provide that certain transfers of assets for "less than fair market value" (that is, what we commonly understand as a gift) will be *counted* as part of the Medicaid applicant's assets unless a "waiting period" has elapsed between the time of the gift and the application for Medicaid.

The effect of this rule is widely misunderstood. For example, if a person makes a gift of say, $20,000 and shortly thereafter applies for Medicaid, the rule against such transfers will *not* cause the $20,000 to be returned to the applicant, nor will any state official go out and confiscate the funds. Rather, the applicant is considered to have the $20,000 still available to him (even though it may *not* be because the donees have spent or dissipated the money, for instance). Therefore, the applicant would not qualify for Medicaid benefits for a period of time or until the funds are "spent down" as discussed later. In effect, the disqualifying gifts are, on paper at least, added back to the applicant's financial statement for purposes of determining his eligibility for Medicaid.

In actual fact, the applicant does *not* have the money, as he has given it away. As far as the Medicaid people are concerned, however, that is not their problem, and the $20,000 must be spent toward the applicant's care or dealt with in some other way (see Chapter 4, "Strategies to Protect Your Assets") before he can qualify for Medicaid. If this were not the rule, everyone could simply give away all his money and immediately qualify for Medicaid.

Do *not* try to illegally hide (or "forget" to report) assets that have been given away by a Medicaid applicant within the thirty-six-month period prior to the application. If they are later discovered by the authorities, you will not only have to pay it all back but you could face a stiff fine and possible jail term for Medicaid fraud. It's not worth it, especially when the transfer can be done legally, as we will see.

Technically, the adding back of transferred assets applies only if it can be shown that the transfer was made for the purpose of becoming eligible for Medicaid benefits. However, unless the applicant can show that the transfer was clearly made *exclusively for some other purpose* than to qualify for Medicaid and the person's admission to a nursing home was unforeseeable, most practitioners accept the waiting period as an unavoidable planning requirement and attempt to work with it.

How Long Must You Wait after a Transfer?

For several years the maximum disqualifying "waiting period" was twenty-four months, and even longer in some states, depending on the amount that was transferred. Then, under MECCA, in 1988 all states were required to apply a thirty-month maximum waiting period for gifts made by the applicant (or his spouse). This changed once again under the 1993 Omnibus Budget Reconciliation Act (OBRA), resulting in a more complicated rule. Since August 10, 1993 (transfers made *after* that date), a *thirty-six-month* waiting period has applied. And for gifts relating to trusts, a *sixty-month* waiting period has applied, though neither of these is a "maximum," as we will see.

A confusing feature of the waiting period is that while it cannot be more than the law provides, it can be *less*. This is because the actual waiting (or disqualification) period is calculated by dividing the amount or value of the gift by the average cost of *private*-pay care in the particular state or region. Every state publishes the applicable figure as part of its Medicaid regulations. For instance, if the state's figure is $3,000 per month, then a gift of $30,000 will disqualify the individual for only *ten* months, and *not* thirty-six months. After the ten-month penalty period, the individual can apply for Medicaid; he would *not* have to wait for thirty or thirty-six months to apply. See Chapter 4 illustrating the "half-a-loaf" strategy, which you can use to save thousands of dollars by giving away less than all of your remaining assets.

When an institutionalized person applies for Medicaid, the state will ask him to report all gifts or other transfers he made within thirty-six months of the application. It will also ask him if he or his spouse *ever* created a trust or if either is the beneficiary of any trust. If the answer to any of these questions is *yes*, then the state will require a copy of the trust, as well as statements of all trust transactions and distributions within sixty months of the application.

For outright gifts or other nontrust transfers that were made more than thirty-six months before the application, there will be no penalty or further waiting period, *regardless* of the size of the gift.

For gifts to or from certain trusts (described below), distributions to third parties (i.e., beneficiaries *other* than the applicant or his spouse) that took place more than sixty months before the application will not require any further waiting period.

Therefore, regardless of the amount of the gift or transfer, the *waiting* period can be no longer than thirty-six or sixty months, but the *penalty* period can be longer. So long as you don't apply before the end of the applicable waiting period (also called a "look-back" period), your gifts or transfers will be safe.

For instance, if the applicant made an outright gift of $300,000, he would only have to wait thirty-six months, as this is the maximum waiting period (but not the maximum disqualification period) for outright gifts, *provided* he didn't make the mistake of applying too soon for Medicaid benefits. (See illustration below.)

Important Note

As indicated above, the waiting period is also a "look-back" period; that is, it is not only prospective but retroactive. This can be a vital difference for gifts that result in more than a thirty-six-month (or sixty-month) disqualification. If this happens and the application for Medicaid is made *even a day too soon,* the results could be catastrophic.

To Illustrate

Katherine makes an outright gift of her $300,000 home (her only asset) to her sister, Marjorie. The average private pay rate in her state is $3,000, and therefore the gift causes a potential disqualification or waiting period of $300,000 ÷ $3,000 per month = 100 months. If Katherine waits until after thirty-six months after the gift to apply for Medicaid, she will qualify. When she is asked the question "Did you make any gifts within the past thirty-six months?" she may honestly answer, "No."

But a slight slip-up can result in disaster: Instead of applying after the thirty-six-month waiting period, Katherine applies just *before* it expires — say, during the last week of the thirty-sixth month. Now the answer to the question on the transfer of assets would be *"Yes,"* since 35 3/4 months ago she transferred the home to Marjorie.

The effect of this slip-up is to *disqualify* Katherine for *one hundred months* from the date of the original transfer!

Look-Back Period for Trusts

For years, various types of trusts have been used to effectively protect family assets from Medicaid grasp, and in some cases, they may still be as effective (see my detailed discussion on trusts in Chapter 4). However, the 1993 OBRA change raised the "price of admission" to a level that not everyone can afford. The increased price is reflected in the new five-year (sixty-month) look-back period that applies to trusts established after August 10, 1993 (though some states may have adopted a later effective date).

Though the trust transfer rules are extremely complicated, the following is a summary of how they work:

Rule 1. Transfers to irrevocable trusts where the trust provides that under no circumstances can any distributions from the trust or from a specified portion of the trust be made to the individual (meaning in this section the person who created the trust) or his spouse: the look-back period is sixty months.

To Illustrate

Harry establishes an irrevocable trust to which he contributes $250,000 worth of 6 percent treasury bonds (the principal). The trust provides that none of the principal may be distributed to him, but that he may receive all of the income (the 6 percent interest) for his life. On his death, the principal passes to his children. Since under no circumstances can the principal be paid to him, this is considered a transfer of assets subject to the sixty-month look-back. It is not clear for Medicaid purposes (though it is eminently clear for tax and substantive law purposes) whether the value of Harry's transfer of principal to the trust should be reduced by the present value of Harry's right to income for his lifetime.

Important Note

Once the transfer to the trust is made and the sixty-month look-back applies, future transfers *out of* the trust are not subject to *any* look-back. Therefore, if two years later, the trustee makes a distribution of $100,000 to Harry's children, there are *no* Medicaid consequences to this distribution.

Rule 2. Transfers to *irrevocable* trusts where some portion of the assets may be distributed to the individual are not considered transfers, and as to that portion there is no look-back period, unless that portion, or part of it, is transferred to a third party. When that happens, the transfer to the third party is subject to a thirty-six-month look-back. Until such a transfer is made, there is no disqualifying transfer because all of the applicable portion is considered to be available to the individual.

To Illustrate (Rule #2)

David establishes an irrevocable trust which provides that the trustee can make discretionary payments of principal and income to David and David's children. On David's death, any remaining balance will pass to his children. About a year after the trust is created, the trustee distributes $75,000 to David's children.

There is no disqualifying transfer on the creation of the trust since all of the trust assets are treated as being available to David (on the basis that the trustee has discretion to pay them all to David). However, the distribution of $75,000 to David's children is a transfer of assets on the date of such distribution and subject to the thirty-six-month look-back from that date.

Rule 3. Transfers to a *revocable* trust are not considered disqualifying transfers because the trust assets may be recovered at any time by the individual simply by revoking the trust. However, transfers *from* the revocable trust to a third party are disqualifying transfers and subject to a look-back period of *sixty* months.

To Illustrate (Rule #3)

Donald establishes a revocable trust for himself and his spouse, naming himself as trustee (though it would not matter who is trustee). Sometime later, he distributes $100,000 out of the trust to his children. The distribution to his children is subject to a sixty-month look-back.

Important Note

Many individuals who adhere to the "do-it-yourself" form of estate planning have so-called trustee bank accounts, where they open an account naming themselves as trustee for a child or another relative. These are considered revocable trusts and not only are all of the balances countable as assets belonging to the trustee for Medicaid purposes, but an inadvertent payment to a "beneficiary" from this account will be a transfer subject to the *sixty-month* look-back.

Important Note

The transfer of assets rule is primarily aimed at individuals who at some point enter a nursing home. Federal law requires states to penalize *institutionalized* individuals for making transfers but does *not* require them to penalize individuals who are not institutionalized. States are given the option of adopting provisions to this effect and it remains to be seen just how many will do so. In the meantime, this means that an uninstitutionalized person could transfer his home and any other assets and immediately apply for (and qualify for) Medicaid. But how much good will this do him? In many states it will allow him to qualify for certain at-home or community service benefits, but not for nursing home benefits. Furthermore, even though a transfer is made before an individual is institutionalized, if he is subsequently institutionalized within the look-back period, it will make no difference that he was not institutionalized at the time of the transfer.

Transfers of the Home

Another important change brought about by MECCA is treatment of transfer of your home. Prior to MECCA, transfer of the home generally would not affect a person's Medicaid eligibility, even if he transferred it just before entering a nursing home. This has dramatically changed.

Now, if a person transfers his home for less than fair value, the transfer will disqualify him from receiving Medicaid benefits for an extended period after the transfer (but see the illustration above), *unless* the transfer is made:

- To the spouse of the applicant
- To a child who is under age twenty-one, blind, or permanently and totally disabled
- To a brother or sister of the applicant who is a co-owner of the home and has been living in the home for at least one year immediately before the applicant's institutionalization
- To a child (or other than a child as described previously) who has been living in the home for at least two years before the applicant's institutionalization and who has provided care for the applicant for a period up to the time of institutionalization, enabling him to stay at home rather than be institutionalized.

In short, the home may be transferred to one or more persons in any of these categories at any time, with *no* waiting period and *without* affecting the transferor's eligibility for Medicaid.

Tip

See comments in Chapter 4 on what to do and what not to do with your home.

Tip

Even under the MECCA rules, except for the home as discussed above, any other *exempt assets* (for example, an automobile) can be transferred by the applicant to anyone at any time (in the absence of fraud or contrivance) without affecting a person's Medicaid eligibility.

Important Note

This does not necessarily mean you can purchase an exempt asset, such as an automobile, and then immediately transfer it to a family member without fear of disqualification. In such a case it is quite likely that the state will (and some states *do*) look at this as a transfer of the money rather than the exempt asset, and you'll have a fight on your hands. (For better ideas, see Chapter 4.)

Tip

If a disqualifying transfer of the home is made and no other solution is available, OBRA rules allow a "cure" of the transfer. That is, if the home is returned to the applicant (and/or his spouse, if there is one), then he may reapply for benefits and qualify as if the transfer was never made. This is an important change in the law, because prior to OBRA, cures were not allowed except in hardship cases and even then not with regularity. (See more discussion on this later in this chapter and again in Chapter 4.)

Serial Transfers

In an effort to circumvent the transfer of assets rules, a scheme was often used which had the effect of reducing the disqualification period by making repeated transfers within the penalty period itself.

This is because the penalty period normally begins on the date of each transfer so that serial transfers would bring about overlapping penalty periods. In many states, this scheme had the effect of rendering a portion or all of the interim transfers without penalty.

For instance, say that Jack made a transfer of $40,000 on January 1, which disqualified him for ten months (assuming the private pay rate for his state was $4,000 per month), or until November 1, of that year. On March 1, however, he made an additional transfer of $20,000. Based on the same measuring rule, this second transfer would disqualify him until August 1 (five months after the transfer). But since he was already disqualified until November, the March transfer is effectively without penalty.

Not anymore.

OBRA 1993 requires the states in such cases to "tack on" to the end of a previous penalty period any "interim" penalty periods resulting from transfers occurring within an existing penalty period. In other words, penalty periods from transfers can no longer run concurrently, and a penalty period caused by an interim transfer will be suspended until other penalty periods have run out. The suspended penalty will begin at that time.

To Illustrate

> Millie makes a gift of $60,000 to her daughter, Julie, on January 1, 1996. The penalty period measuring amount in her state is $4,000 per month, so the transfer will disqualify her for $60,000 ÷ $4,000, or fifteen months, or until April 1, 1997. On August 1, 1996, Millie makes another transfer, of $20,000, which disqualifies her for four months. However, the second disqualification period cannot begin until the first disqualification period has expired. Therefore, the four-month disqualification from the second (August 1st) transfer will begin to run on April 1, 1997, when the first period runs out.

Transfers by or Between Spouses

MECCA makes another important exception to disqualifying transfers. That is, transfers of countable assets from the applicant *to his spouse* are not considered disqualifying because of the pooling of assets requirement. In other words, what difference will it make to the state if a husband gives all his assets to his wife if his wife's assets are counted along with his own? It should be noted that the applicant-to-spouse transfer exception does not then give the spouse the opportunity to freely transfer assets she received from the applicant. In fact, the law provides that she cannot even transfer *her own* assets without risking disqualification of her spouse as a result of *her* transfer. As will be seen later, however, transfers between spouses still offer important planning opportunities to preserve family assets.

Transfers to Trusts for Disabled Children

Another exception to the disqualifying transfer rules was added by the 1993 OBRA change. Prior to OBRA, a parent could make a transfer *to* a disabled child but, for some unknown reason, *not* to a trust for that child. OBRA now allows parents to establish and fund a trust for a child who is blind or totally and permanently disabled. The trust must be "solely for the benefit of the child," apparently meaning that no one but the child may benefit from the trust. Nevertheless, it seems to leave enough leeway to design a trust that will preserve family assets for the disabled child and allow what is left to pass ultimately to the other members of the family. (See Chapter 4 for more details.) Transfers to such a trust will not be subject to the disqualification rules.

Transfers to Trusts for Disabled Applicants under Sixty-five

This exception, also brought about by OBRA, allows transfers to a trust for the *applicant* himself, if the applicant is *under sixty-five* and permanently disabled (under the Social Security rules), *but only* if the trust is established by the applicant's guardian, parent, grandparent, or by a court (i.e., NOT by the applicant himself). Further, on the applicant's death, any funds remaining in the trust must first be applied to repay the state for all Medicaid benefits paid by the state on behalf of the applicant/beneficiary. If there are assets over this amount, they may pass to other family members.

> Although at first glance this arrangement may appear unattractive, there can be cases where it can nevertheless save substantial amounts. This is because the state usually pays considerably less than private pay patients for the same services and care. Therefore, such a trust would indirectly allow the individual to get the state's "discount" on the costs of his care, use the funds in the meantime, then pay the state back, interest free, when he dies (for more detail see Chapter 4).

Transfers Intended to Be for Fair Value (That Are Not)

The limited value of this exception speaks for itself and would appear to apply where the applicant, accidentally and in good faith, receives something valued less than the asset was actually worth. Again, it offers little or no planning advantage since it is unlikely to happen. For instance, a person is not likely to sell a $100,000 home to a third party for $50,000. But if he does so in good faith and without intending to make a gift of the difference, the exception would apply. On the other hand, if the "sale" is to a family member, it is highly unlikely that the state Medicaid agency would buy the story. Instead, the "sale" would be treated as a disqualifying transfer of $50,000, the difference between the fair value and the price paid.

Transfers Resulting in "Undue Hardship"

No doubt we could easily argue that any denial of benefits would work an undue hardship on our families, since it would mean we would have to pay thousands in nursing home costs, but this is definitely not what Congress had in mind under the undue hardship exception. Nevertheless, if it is determined that denial of benefits because of the transfer would result in "undue hardship" to the individual, the state must grant benefits, despite the otherwise disqualifying transfer.

Undue hardship exists when a denial of benefits "would deprive the individual of medical care such that his or her health or life would be endangered." Undue hardship also exists when denial of benefits "would deprive the individual of food, clothing, shelter or other necessities of life."

These standards are imposed quite strictly and the states have considerable leeway in interpreting them. It does not include, for example, a need to change one's lifestyle because he or members of his family now have to pay for nursing home care due to a disqualifying transfer of assets. States can also *require* that the individual make an effort to recover the transferred assets before the hardship exception will be allowed.

In any event, the state *is required*
• to give the applicant notice that an undue hardship exception exists
• to provide a timely process to determine whether an undue hardship exception exists
• to provide a process under which the applicant can appeal a state's denial to grant him an undue hardship exception.

Returning Assets to the Individual: A "Cure"

Under prior law, once an individual made a disqualifying transfer, he started a penalty period that could not be undone. If it turned out that the transfer was ill-advised or even unintentional (as a disqualification), it didn't matter. The individual was generally out of luck and had to wait out the disqualification period. Now, however, OBRA allows individuals to *cure* a disqualifying transfer by returning the transferred asset (or its value) to the individual. This allows the opportunity to save where none existed before (see Chapter 4). It does require, however, that the planning *start* from the return of the asset.

To Illustrate

On January 1, Bickford makes a gift of his home, worth $160,000 (which constitutes all of his assets over $2,000), to his daughter, Becky. The average private pay rate in his state is $4,000 per month, so Bickford is disqualified for forty months. In late June, Bickford enters a nursing home and applies for Medicaid. He is told of his penalty period but finds that he simply has no funds to pay for his care. Becky then transfers the home back to Bickford. Since the home is an exempt asset while owned by Bickford, and since Becky has *cured* the disqualifying transfer, Bickford will qualify for Medicaid as of the date he entered the nursing home.

Note

The cure can operate to qualify the individual for Medicaid or at least allow the opportunity to "correct" an error and start again. See Chapter 4 on some important planning ideas when applying the cure.

Disclaimers

Occasionally (and unfortunately, not infrequently), it happens that an individual on Medicaid becomes entitled to receive assets which, if he accepts them, will immediately disqualify him from receiving Medicaid. In the typical case, for instance, a relative of the elderly individual will die, naming the individual as a beneficiary under a *will*, or the relative will die without a *will* and the elderly individual will be an heir entitled to a share of the estate. What to do?

In the past, some states have allowed the Medicaid beneficiary to *disclaim* the inheritance, and the individual's Medicaid benefits would not be affected. A disclaimer is a legal rejection of the inheritance or other benefit before it is received or enjoyed. In most cases, a disclaimer must be filed within nine months of the date of death, or if a trust or other gift, nine months from the time the trust or gift becomes irrevocable. If properly made, the disclaimer causes the gift or inheritance to be treated as if it were never made to or received by the disclaiming individual. Many states, on the other hand, treated the disclaimer itself as a disqualifying transfer of the rejected share.

Now OBRA 1993 has made this the law: If a person disclaims an asset, it is treated as if the person received it, then gave it away, presumably as of the date of the disclaimer, though this is not yet clear. Therefore, if an individual on Medicaid becomes entitled to an inheritance or other gift, it will be necessary to plan to dispose of that asset in a manner that will least affect the continuation of the individual's Medicaid benefits (see Chapter 4). *Note* that an inheritance from an estate generally is not considered an asset for Medicaid purposes until the individual actually receives it from the executor, or until the executor makes it available to him.

In summary, in order to prevent people from simply giving their money or property away to a family member just before or after entering a nursing home so that they can have their nursing home bills paid by Medicaid and still protect the family assets, the government has enacted laws that disqualify applicants from receiving benefits if they make such gifts. Basically, the rule is that if you make a gift you may not be eligible to receive Medicaid for up to thirty-six months after the gift (and sixty months in the case of certain trusts). And because of the "pooling of assets" rule between spouses, if *either* spouse makes a gift, *both* can be disqualified for up to thirty-six (or sixty) months, regardless of which one enters a nursing home.

There are the basic rules. Now we should take a look at what strategies we can use to work with them legally and still protect our assets.

CHAPTER FOUR

Strategies to Protect Your Assets

*A*lthough you may be tempted to do so, it is not a good idea to read this chapter before all the others, as it can lead to some confusion and a possible misunderstanding or misapplication of the strategies. It is important, for instance, that you understand the differences between an *exempt* asset, a *countable* asset, and an *inaccessible* asset before taking any steps. You should also understand the pooling of spousal assets rule, the spousal resource allowance, and how jointly held assets are treated, all explained earlier. It is equally important that you understand what assets can be transferred (and under what circumstances) without affecting eligibility, and how long you must wait after a transfer before you apply for Medicaid. Since so much is at stake (usually your home and life's savings), it can be dangerous to take any shortcuts.

The first thing to remember is that virtually any gifts of countable assets (except to a spouse) will trigger all or a portion of the thirty-six- or sixty-month disqualification rules unless it can be shown (not very likely) that the gifts were made *exclusively* for a purpose other than to qualify for Medicaid. Similarly, even the home, which is an exempt asset, can cause disqualification if it is transferred to anyone other than one or more of the four allowable transferees (that is, a spouse, an adult child who has lived in the home for two years and cared for the parent during some or all of that time, a sibling co-owner who has lived in the home for a year, or a minor or permanently disabled child). Furthermore, a transfer of the home to a trust by an institutionalized person will make the home a *countable* asset, even though the trust may be revocable.

Important Note — The $10,000 "Tax-Free" Gift

> Many people are under the mistaken impression that it is permissible to make gifts of up to $10,000 to various family members without affecting Medicaid eligibility. *This is not so!* The misunderstanding stems from a confusion of the federal gift tax laws (which allow "tax-free" annual gifts of $10,000 per donee) with the Medicaid laws (which allow virtually no gifts at all). Therefore, simply stated: (1) if any gifts are to be made, they *must* be structured to fall under one of the exceptions or strategies discussed later, or else you must be prepared to wait out the required penalty period before applying for Medicaid benefits, and (2) the $10,000 gift limitation *does not apply* to Medicaid planning.

Gifts of Exempt Assets

With the exception of the home (which is covered separately in this chapter), a gift of an exempt asset (as defined in Chapter 2) can basically be made to anyone at any time without affecting Medicaid eligibility. This is because even if the gift were returned to the applicant, he would still be eligible for Medicaid, since the gifted asset was not countable in the first place. There are situations, however, where caution should be exercised in making gifts of exempt assets.

Say that John is ill and has about $25,000 in savings. He uses $23,000 of the savings to purchase an automobile (which is exempt), and a couple of weeks later, while in the process of applying for Medicaid, he makes a gift of the auto to his son. Although John technically qualifies for Medicaid, under these conditions you can be almost certain that the state will attack the purchase and the immediate transfer of the auto as a "step transaction" and will treat it simply as a disqualifying gift of $23,000 to John's son. It would have been much more advisable for John to simply keep the car for a period of time, and perhaps at some future date transfer it to his son, or simply arrange that the son have a survivorship interest in the auto on John's death. Or perhaps better still, use the half-a-loaf plan discussed below.

Other than the risk of a step transaction as described, exempt assets, aside from the home, may be freely transferred without affecting Medicaid eligibility.

The Half-a-Loaf Plan

Remember that in all states the disqualification or penalty period must be based on the amount given away divided by the average cost of private pay nursing home care in the area. Accordingly, if a person makes a $12,000 gift and the average cost of care in her area (published by the local Medicaid agency) is $4,000 per month, then she is disqualified for a period of three months ($12,000 ÷ $4,000 per month). After the three-month period, she may qualify for Medicaid, assuming she has no other countable assets.

An interesting characteristic of this rule, and the characteristic that gives rise to an important planning opportunity, is that the rule only looks at what has been given away, and not at what is retained. This allows a person to give away a portion of her assets and retain a portion which will provide for her care during the disqualification period arising from the gift. If calculated correctly, the result is to save the entire amount given away and eventually qualify for Medicaid.

To Illustrate

Marjorie, a widow, has $80,000 and no other assets. She is about to enter a nursing home and would like to save some of this money for her son, Max. The average net cost of private pay care in her area is $4,000 per month, and it turns out that will also be the cost of her care in the nursing home. If Marjorie makes a gift of $40,000 to her son, this will disqualify her for ten months ($40,000 ÷ $4,000 per month). However, she has *retained* $40,000, which will carry her for the disqualification period. Once that is spent and ten months have gone by, Marjorie will qualify for Medicaid, and she has saved $40,000 for her son.

Important Note

Calculations for the half-a-loaf strategy can be tricky. The measuring cost of care to determine the penalty period may be more or less than the actual cost. Furthermore, if the individual has income, such as a pension or Social Security, this must be factored in, along with necessary expenses, such as the cost of medical insurance (Medex, Blue Cross, etc.). If the individual is not yet in a nursing home and it is unknown just when she will enter one, the plan becomes almost total guess work. In short, it is usually a plan of last resort, when a person is either about to enter a nursing home or is already institutionalized.

To Illustrate

In our example above Marjorie still has her $80,000 and is just about to enter the nursing home. She has income of $1,200 per month from a pension and Social Security. Her necessary expenses are $200 per month, which includes her health insurance premiums, leaving a net amount of $1,000 per month, which can be applied toward her care. If Marjorie gives away $45,000, this will disqualify her for just over eleven months ($45,000 ÷ $4,000 per month). The gift will leave her with $35,000, which at a cost of $3,000 per month for her care, will more than cover her care for the eleven-month disqualification period.

If there is a spouse involved, the half-a-loaf plan would be carried out *after* the snapshot is taken and *after* the spousal resource allowance is determined. Otherwise, the healthy spouse may be reducing her spousal resource allowance.

To Illustrate

Betty and Mario have $100,000 and they give away $20,000, leaving them with $80,000. Then Mario enters a nursing home and the state determines Betty's spousal resource allowance to be one-half of $80,000, or $40,000. If Mario had waited until *after* the snapshot to make the gift, Betty's allowance would have been $50,000, and yet the same disqualification period would apply.

Note

The half-a-loaf plan is not restricted to cash gifts. A person could give away a fractional interest in a home or other property. The share would be valued (perhaps at a discount?) at the "fair market value" at the time of the gift, and the disqualification period would be based on the value of the gifted share.

Very Important Note

Once you make a gift under the half-a-loaf plan, the disqualification period begins and (except in the case of a return of funds) *does not stop until it expires.* This means that you must be prepared to carry the costs of care during that period. Unless there are funds remaining in the name of the institutionalized person *after* the period is over, you should *NOT* use any of the retained funds to buy a burial contract, cemetery plot, or any other noncare expenditure.

Planning after a Cure

As discussed in Chapter 3, an individual can "cure" a disqualifying transfer of assets by receiving the assets (or their fair value) back, effectively placing him in the same position as if he never made the transfer. If the transferred asset was his *home*, the re-transfer of the home may allow him to immediately qualify or even retroactively qualify for Medicaid, since the home is generally an exempt asset. If the transferred asset was countable, however, a re-transfer will only serve to stop the earlier disqualification period. At the same time, however, it will cause his continued disqualification because he now has excess assets. Another important provision in the federal rules indicates that a return of only a portion of the transferred assets will reduce the disqualification period proportionally. Together, these rules offer the opportunity to save from that point.

To Illustrate _____

> Example 1. Harley transferred $80,000 to his daughter. The average private pay cost in their state is $4,000 per month. Ten months after the transfer, Harley's daughter becomes institutionalized and his daughter gives back the $80,000. This stops the disqualification period but now Harley must find a way to dispose of some or all of the $80,000. Under the half-a-loaf method Harley could give away $40,000 and save $40,000 to cover himself during the ensuing ten-month period.
>
> Example 2. Same facts as above except that instead of giving the full $80,000, Harley's daughter only gives him back $40,000. This is because ten months have already gone by since the initial transfer, so Harley has "used up" $40,000 worth of the original disqualifying transfers ($4,000 per month × ten months). Therefore, Harley, now institutionalized, has only $40,000 of excess assets to contend with. Again applying the half-a-loaf method, Harley gives $20,000 to his daughter and is disqualified for five months from that transfer ($20,000 ÷ $4,000 per month). However, he has kept $20,000 to carry him through that period.
>
> The result in Example 2 is that his daughter ends up with $40,000 plus $20,000, or $60,000 protected from Medicaid — a savings of an additional $20,000 over the first example.

Creation or Purchase of Exempt Assets

When a family is faced with the prospect of nursing home costs, one of the most important things to do, as *soon* as possible, is to take a financial assessment of the countable versus noncountable assets belonging to the applicant and/or his spouse (including any large gifts that they have made within the previous three-year period). Countable assets, to the extent reasonable and possible, should then be disposed of in a manner that will not jeopardize Medicaid benefits. Unfortunately, for assets that clearly belong to the applicant or his spouse, this is not easy to do without triggering the thirty-six-month wait, unless, instead of "disposing" of them, we simply *change their character* from countable to noncountable.

Very Important Note _____

The rule prohibiting transfers of assets simply prohibits transfers without adequate consideration. In other words, *if you get something of equal value in return for the assets you have transferred, you have not violated the rule,* even though the item you received was not a countable asset.

To Illustrate _____

Philip, a widower, has a home and about $45,000 in savings. The home has a mortgage on it with a balance of $41,000. Philip is about to enter a nursing home. If Philip uses $41,000 of his savings to pay off his mortgage and puts an additional $2,000 into a burial account, he will immediately qualify for Medicaid. Payment of the mortgage and purchase of the burial account are considered transfers for full consideration, so *no penalty* applies.

Important Note _____

In the above illustration, if Philip did *not* pay off his mortgage, he would *not* qualify for Medicaid until he spent all but $2,000 of his $45,000 in savings. The state looks only at total countable assets; it does not consider or allow a deduction for any debts you may have.

Other examples of legally converting countable assets into noncountable assets include the use of funds to construct an addition to your home, or a new bathroom, garage, or driveway, or to install wall-to-wall carpeting, or, as stated earlier, to purchase a car. All of these options should definitely be considered *before* an application of Medicaid is made.

You may also apply funds to the costs of maintenance and upkeep of any other assets and, of course, for your care, if appropriate. Payment for any services rendered to you, such as housekeeping, grounds maintenance, home repairs, and so on, are all quite permissible, but be careful about paying *children* for their services, or "reimbursing" them for funds they "loaned" to you, as discussed later.

Annuities

There is yet another tactic used to protect assets by converting them, but the conversion in this case is to *income* rather than into exempt assets. You may recall that for Medicaid purposes, income is counted somewhat differently than assets. For instance, a single person who has $10,000 of countable assets will not qualify for Medicaid, but a single person who has $500 per month of income but no assets would qualify. Therefore, if the person with $10,000 used this money to purchase the right to receive income of $500 per month for a certain number of years or, in some cases, for his lifetime, he could qualify immediately for Medicaid. This conversion of the countable asset to income is generally accomplished through the purchase of an annuity.

In its purest form, an annuity is an annual payment during a person's lifetime. In the typical case, a person will purchase an *annuity contract* from an insurance company. The contract will provide for a guaranteed payment (often on a monthly basis) for the rest of the person's lifetime. Of course, the payments are based on the person's life expectancy and the insurance company's rate of return. The insurance company is taking the risk that the person will outlive her expectancy (since it has to keep on paying no matter how long the person lives), while the purchaser is risking that she could die "too soon," since all payments stop on her death under a "pure" annuity. For this reason, insurance companies offer an alternative, called a "term certain" annuity.

A term certain annuity guarantees that payments will be made at least for the specified term, but if the "annuitant" (the person on whose life the contract is measured, and usually the one who receives the payments) lives beyond the term, payments will continue until her death.

To Illustrate

Maria, age seventy-five, purchases an annuity which will pay her $750 per month for the rest of her life, but with a term certain of nine years. She names her daughter, Rita, as beneficiary. If Maria dies one year after payments begin, then Rita will receive the $750 per month for the balance of the nine-year period. But if Maria dies in the tenth year, no further payments will be made.

As noted above, the purchase of an annuity can effectively convert a countable asset (the funds or other property used to acquire the annuity) into income. In many cases, this can result in immediate Medicaid eligibility. This type of purchase is allowed on the basis that the purchaser is making a transfer for valid consideration.

Important Note

Not all annuity purchases will qualify as transfers for valid consideration. The government's position is that the annuity must be "actuarially sound." That is, the expected return must be based on the amount paid, amortized over a reasonable estimate of the annuitant's life expectancy. Usually this is only of concern where a term certain contract is used, but except for the case of private annuities (discussed below), a term certain would almost always be used. Briefly, it can be stated this way: If the term certain is greater than the annuitant's reasonable life expectancy, then a part of the purchase is likely to be a disqualifying transfer.

To Illustrate

In our example above, Maria, age seventy-five, has a life expectancy of just over nine years. If Maria purchases an annuity with a term certain of fifteen years, a portion of the purchase will be deemed to be a disqualifying transfer to Rita.

Annuities can be especially valuable where spouses are involved and one has to unexpectedly enter a nursing home. If nothing is done, the spouses may be forced to spend most of their savings toward long-term care, leaving the at-home spouse with only around $75,000. If instead, the at-home spouse uses the "spend-down" funds to purchase an annuity for herself, the institutionalized spouse could immediately qualify for Medicaid. (These arrangements are illustrated in greater detail in Case Studies eight and nine in Chapter 11.)

Note

Although, generally, one purchases an annuity from an insurance company (a commercial annuity), it is also possible to purchase an annuity from another *person* (a *"private"* annuity).

A private annuity is an annuity contract between two parties, neither of which is an insurance company or a large pension plan. Typically, the private annuity will be between members of the same family.

To Illustrate

Agnes's only asset consists of about $50,000 worth of telephone stock. At age eighty-one, she has become infirm and is likely to enter a nursing home within the next several months. Because she has excess assets, Agnes cannot qualify for Medicaid. To remedy this, Agnes enters into a written contract with her niece, providing that Agnes will transfer to her niece all her telephone stock, and in return the niece will pay to Agnes $600 per month for the rest of Agnes's life. This is a private annuity, and if properly structured (and calculated) it will result in Agnes's qualifying for Medicaid because, although she has income, she has no assets. (But remember, she will have to use the monthly income to pay for her care.)

Tip

An important practical difference between a private annuity and a commercial annuity is that, generally, the private annuity should *not* have a term certain. This is because an early death will simply benefit the family member who was paying the annuity. There would be no need to continue payments for a specified period.

Important Note _____

The tax and legal aspects of private annuities are very complicated and expert advice is positively essential in such cases. (For reference to IRS treatment of private annuities see Revenue Rulings 69-74 and 55-119.) Further, your state's laws should first be checked to be sure that private annuity contracts are permissible. (Some states' laws provide that annuities can be sold only by registered insurance companies.)

Warning _____

The purchase of an annuity, whether commercial or private, to convert assets to income, especially between spouses, is a tactic that will undoubtedly become extremely popular, largely because it works so well in special situations and is clearly allowable under the law. Therefore, be prepared for an attempt to change the law to close this loophole. Annuities purchased prior to a change in the law should be safe.

Paying Children or Other Relatives for Services Rendered

As explained earlier, a transfer of assets in return for fair consideration is not considered a "disqualifying" transfer. The use of assets to purchase or pay for *services* should also fall under this category of permissible expenditures, and, in most cases, it does. Questions clearly arise, however, when applicants pay *relatives* for services rendered, as the freedom to make such payments without question would invite tremendous abuse.

Payments to a child or other relative of the Medicaid applicant may be suspect, partly because, in the usual case, children or other close relatives normally perform all types of services for their parents as gestures of love or just out of a sense of familial responsibility. To open the door for permissible transfers (in the form of payment for services) in every such case would allow a family to quickly drain off its available assets and qualify for Medicaid on the pretext that the applicant was simply paying family members for "services rendered." For this reason, most states consider such services gratuitous or provided in exchange for love and affection. Unless there is strong evidence to support an agreement to pay *prior* to the rendering of services, the states are extremely strict about allowing payment to close relatives for services rendered, though such payments are by no means impermissible.

The law and regulations provide that payments for services to a "non–legally responsible person" are permissible, provided, of course, that the payment reflects "fair value" for services rendered. Fair value is generally measured by objective community standards and, although never precise, is not difficult to establish. For instance, if three contractors estimate a range of $1,200 to $1,800 to paint a house, something within that range ought to be acceptable. In any event, you should be well prepared to document the work done and the fairness of the amount paid.

A non–legally responsible person is one who is not legally obliged to provide support for the person in question. In most instances, spouses are legally responsible for each other (until one enters a nursing home), and a parent is legally responsible for a minor child. Therefore, a parent could not, for example, charge the child for providing care, maintaining the household, and so on, even though the cost of such services is measurable by community standards.

The responsibility of a child (or other close relative) toward the parent/applicant poses another question. The federal Medicaid law allows states to require children to support their parents (and in fact, such laws are on the books in a number of states, though not actively enforced), but such payments (by the children) will be counted as assets only if payment is actually received by the applicant. Therefore, it appears that children (or other relatives) could render services to an applicant and charge for those services. If this is done, however, great care must be taken to ensure that the transaction is legitimate; otherwise you will face not only countability of the transferred funds (for Medicaid eligibility purposes) but, given the current general attitude of the states toward families who aggressively transfer assets, you could also face *fraud* charges.

To Illustrate _____

> A child who has been providing a service (shopping, cleaning, and so on) for a parent for years without charge may have difficulty convincing the state that he suddenly decided to charge $200 per week for his services. This is not to say that payment for such service is illegal and will automatically be disallowed, only that it almost certainly will be questioned.

In summary, there is no clear rule on the issue, but the standard is this: If the services rendered are valid, the payment fair, and there was a clear agreement, *before* the services were provided, that payment would be made, and if the person who rendered the services had no legal responsibility to do so, payment may be allowed. On the other hand, it will be a waste of your time and could even lead to more trouble if you attempt to qualify for Medicaid by making payments for fabricated service or by making excessive payments for questionable services. Lastly, remember that payments to children for services will be *taxable income* to the child.

Reimbursing Children or Other Relatives for Expenses or Loans

Reimbursement for valid expenses (which are often viewed as loans as far as the children and parents are concerned) should not be as much of a problem as payment for services, as discussed previously, but you should keep in mind that *all* such financial transactions between a parent and child will be scrutinized carefully by the state.

Tip _____

> If a child gives funds to a parent to improve the home, pay for care, or pay a bill, the use of the funds should be *carefully documented as a loan* as should the transfer of the funds from the child to the parent. When possible, the parent should sign a simple promissory note. If this is "uncomfortable" or impossi-

ble, the child should obtain some form of acknowledgment of receipt of the funds and a statement of the parent's intent to repay him or her, such as a brief letter from the parent to the child. Even where no note or letter is available, however, it is still possible to show by the facts and circumstances that it was appropriate for the child to advance the funds and that the child clearly did it with the expectation of reimbursement at some future date.

Problems can also arise when a child advances funds to a parent to improve or maintain a home in which the parent has only a life estate, or a home that is later transferred to the child, sometimes shortly after the improvements.

In the case of a life estate advancement of funds to the parent to *maintain or repair* the home would be appropriate, as this is the parent's obligation as a life tenant. However, as a general rule, *improvements* are the responsibility of the child (who will receive the property on the death of the parent). Therefore, be very careful to distinguish between the two in such cases. (See my detailed discussion on life estates in the section that follows on what to do and what not to do with your home.)

To Illustrate

If a child advances funds to improve a home in which he or she already holds a remainder interest, the state will likely take the position that the child is improving his or her own property. Therefore, a "repayment" by the parent to the child of the advanced funds would probably be viewed by the state as a disqualifying transfer of funds by the parent.

When the home belongs to the parent (that is, there is no life estate), any funds used to improve the home are the responsibility of the parent, and the expense would not, by itself, be considered a disqualifying transfer. Further, it should have no bearing on the parent's decision at some later date to transfer the home to the children (having in mind the applicable waiting period).

Be careful about borrowing to make improvements just before transferring the home to a child. For instance, it is quite likely that borrowing from a child to make a major improvement on the parent's home followed shortly thereafter by a transfer of the home to that child would be viewed as an exception to the rule, and the "repayment" of the loan would correspondingly be viewed as a disqualifying transfer of funds by the parent.

Protecting Assets by Purchasing a Home

Perhaps the largest opportunity for conversion of a countable to a noncountable asset is the purchase of a home. Though it is admittedly somewhat extreme, under the right circumstances it can save the entire family fortune.

To Illustrate

Say that John and Mary have about $300,000 of assets (equally owned), but do not own a home. They live off the income from the $300,000. John is ill and about to enter a nursing home. Before he does, however, John and Mary spend $235,000 to purchase the condo they have been living in, leaving them with $65,000. When John enters the nursing home, their "snapshot" will show only $65,000 of countable assets, and because it is the only source of Mary's income, it is likely that she will be allowed to keep the whole amount. If they had done nothing, their countable assets would have been $300,000, of which Mary would have been allowed to keep only around $75,000. In effect, the plan saved them about $225,000!

Tip

If you use this tactic to protect countable assets, be sure you can show that the applicant or his spouse actually moved into the home and occupied it as a principal residence. It is also conceivable that an applicant could be in a nursing home while his spouse purchased and moved into a new home on her own. In this case, the fact that the ill spouse never occupied the new home should not be a problem. Further, in the case of spouses, it is important to take title in the sole name of the at-home spouse. (For more illustrations of strategies to protect assets, see the case studies in Chapter 11.)

What to Do with Joint Assets

In the typical family, spouses have a habit of placing everything they own in their joint names, regardless of which spouse contributed the funds. Under the Medicaid rules, this is no longer significant, because, in effect, the assets and transfers of one spouse are treated as attributable to the other. Therefore, where spouses are concerned, strategies for jointly held assets will be the same as those for assets held individually by a spouse.

As to the assets held jointly by the applicant and someone other than a spouse, some very different rules apply. First, as to joint bank accounts, the rules start with the presumption that *all* of the funds in such accounts belong to the Medicaid applicant. It is up to the nonapplicant joint owner to prove that he or she had contributed his or her own separate funds to that account.

When the nonapplicant did not contribute funds to the joint account, any withdrawals will be deemed to be transfers by the applicant.

As to assets other than bank accounts, you may have a better chance. Where stocks, bonds, real estate, and so on, are *registered* in joint names by the applicant and someone other than a spouse, Medicaid laws assume that each joint tenant owns a proportionate share of the asset.

To Illustrate

Irving has a savings account containing $20,000, shares of stock worth $30,000, and a vacation home worth $100,000, all in joint names with his daughter, Joanne. At this point, Irving's countable assets will presumably include the entire bank account, but only *one-half* the value of the stocks and *one-half* the value of the summer home.

In such cases, unless there is some other agreement, each joint owner has a legal right to half (if there are only two owners) of the asset and, in fact, could force a severance of the asset (that is, a legal division or a sale) and recover half of the proceeds. Effectively, there was a gift of a share of the asset and this is where the problem may lie. If the joint ownership in the asset was created within thirty-six months of the application for Medicaid benefits, isn't this a disqualifying gift of one-half the value of the asset?

To Illustrate

In January 1995 Dad purchased $200,000 worth of securities, placing them in his name and Daughter's name as joint owners. In March of the same year, he is institutionalized and applies for Medicaid. Is he considered to have $100,000 of assets or something more? Dad is considered to have $100,000 worth of assets but he is also considered to have made a disqualifying transfer to Daughter in the amount of $100,000.

If the nonapplicant is entitled to a share of the joint asset, then the asset should immediately be split to segregate the share that belongs to the applicant. Once the funds or assets are segregated, you must then develop and follow applicable strategies to protect the exposed funds, such as the purchase of exempt assets, half-a-loaf gift, creation of trusts, and so on.

What to Do (and What *Not* to Do) with Your Home

Since the home is usually the most valuable and, for emotional reasons, the most important asset a family has, most homeowners with families are especially concerned about protecting this asset in the event they are faced with long term care costs. Even though the home is considered an exempt asset, it may not remain exempt (for example, where one spouse dies and the other is in a nursing home). Briefly, the options available to a family are as follows:

1. Selling the home (usually) to children

2. Making a gift of the home

3. Making a gift of the home with a reserved life estate

4. Placing the home in a trust

Each of these options will be examined separately, as will a fifth issue: what to do with an *out-of-state* home.

Selling the Home to Children

About the *worst* thing you can do from the standpoint of preserving assets in the face of nursing home costs is to sell the home to your children. Remember, in most cases the home is a noncountable asset. If you sell the home to your children, you would be converting it to a *fully countable asset* (the money or promissory notes you would receive on the sale), which would immediately disqualify you from receiving Medicaid benefits. Further, if your gain on the sale exceeds $125,000, you would also have to pay federal and state capital gains taxes on the excess.

Tip

For some reason, many people have it in their minds that they should not pass up the opportunity to take advantage of the $125,000 capital gains tax exclusion allowed when a person over age fifty-five sells his or her home. So they sell their home to their children for a price ranging from true fair market value down to $125,000. There is absolutely *no reason* to feel that you *must* take the over-fifty-five exclusion. You will not lose any tax dollars by passing it up, and, where Medicaid planning is concerned, it is positively a bad idea, as I have just explained.

Important Note

A "sale" for one dollar is *not* a sale! It is a *gift,* unless the thing you sold is worth only one dollar. Do *not* try to play those games with such a valuable asset as your home.

Making a Gift of the Home to Children

Not quite as bad as a sale, but still not the best option in most cases, is making a gift of the home to your children. By making an outright gift, you actually lose the right to live in the home, and you expose yourself to the possible misfortunes of the child or children who now own the home.

To Illustrate

To "preserve" his home in case he later became ill, Frank made a gift of his home to his son, Rico. As a result of a bad business deal, Rico was sued and his creditor attached the home. After the creditor obtained a judgment against Rico, he obtained a court-ordered sale of the home to pay the judgment. Frank could do absolutely nothing about it and lost the home.

In short, if you make an outright gift of your home to a child (or children) who was sued, or engaged in a bitter divorce, or died, the home could easily be attached, and even sold from under you.

Another problem with an outright gift is that it is likely to succeed in removing the property from your estate for federal and state estate tax purposes. This may sound like a benefit to you (actually it won't matter to you, since you won't be here), but, in fact, it is quite disadvantageous to your children. In most Medicaid-sensitive families, the estate is only of moderate size — maybe $100,000 to $500,000. In such estates, there will be *no* federal estate taxes and even in those states that levy an estate tax, only a relatively small state estate tax, if any. One of the advantages for beneficiaries of any estate is that they inherit estate property with a "stepped-up" cost basis. That is, for purposes of determining their capital gain on a later sale of the property, they use the estate tax value of the inherited property as their cost for the property, even though no estate taxes may be due. Contrast this with the tax rules applying to a person who receives a *gift* of property: generally he uses the *same cost basis* as that of the person who gave him the gift.

To Illustrate

> Say that your home cost you $50,000 twenty years ago but is now worth $300,000. A *gift* of the home to your children and a subsequent sale by them would produce a capital gain to them of $250,000 (ignoring the cost of any home improvements). On the other hand, if the children *inherited* the home when it was worth $300,000, a subsequent sale by them at that price would produce *no* capital gain. Without considering the state estate tax on the inheritance, we're talking about a tax savings to the children in the vicinity of $75,000!

As to gift taxes, this is usually an unnecessary concern, because no federal gift taxes will apply until a person's cumulative taxable lifetime gifts (over $10,000 per person per year) exceed $600,000. And for spouses this amount can be doubled! Therefore, in the types of cases contemplated in this discussion, the question of gift taxes is positively *not* a concern.

Finally, don't forget that a transfer of the home by gift will trigger the thirty-six-month wait under the Medicaid rules unless the transfer falls under one of the exceptions described in the section on transfers of the home in Chapter 3.

Making a Gift of the Home with a Reserved Life Estate

Under the right circumstances, making a gift of the home with a reserved life estate can give you both the legal advantages of the gift and the tax advantages of keeping the property. But first, it is important to remember, as noted previously, that under the Medicaid rules, a gift of the home (*including* a gift with a reserved life estate) will trigger the thirty-six-month wait *unless* the transfer falls under one of the exceptions. However, if neither spouse expects to be in a nursing home within that period, the waiting period should not be a problem.

A life estate is simply the right to occupy and use property during a person's lifetime. Therefore, when you make a gift with a reserved life estate, your donees (in this case, your children) do not have any right to use or occupy the property until *after* your death. If you and your spouse reserve *joint* life estates, then the children will have no rights of use or occupancy until after the death of the survivor of you. In the meantime, however, you have made a legal and irrevocable gift of the "remainder" (what is left after you're gone) to the children. (In legal jargon, they are called the "remaindermen.") In effect, a life estate is a way to keep the property while giving it away.

Although your children, as owners, could sell their remainder interest in the home, any buyer would have to wait until you were both deceased (if a joint life estate) before he could take possession of the property. Therefore, a sale during either of your lives would be highly unlikely without your consent. But even if one did take place, your life estate would *not* be affected.

To Illustrate

Max and Ellen own their home and a moderate amount of savings. One of their main concerns is to pass their home along to their children, since Max and Ellen have worked all their lives for it. Although Max and Ellen are both now in good health, they are concerned that if both of them ended up in nursing homes, the state would eventually take the home. (Remember, the Medicaid recipient's home is exempt only if it is either his principal residence or if a spouse or dependent family member is living there. Thereafter, the state can force a sale of the Medicaid recipient's share to recover benefits paid — see Chapter 8.) Max and Ellen decide to give the home to their two children and reserve the right to live in the home for the rest of their lives. After they make the gift and record the deed, their son Mel is in need of funds and arranges a sale of his remainder interest in one-half the home at far less than its fair value. Although this initially upsets Max and Ellen, they discover that the new owner and any new owner after him will be required to just sit and wait until *both* Max and Ellen are deceased before he can get anything.

Tip

If a sale of the home is anticipated while either spouse is alive, a gift with a reserved life estate is probably *not* a good idea, because the *children* will have to pay a capital gains tax on their share of the gain, based on the portion that relates to their remainder interest. In most cases, the tax on a sale of the remainder interest can be quite significant, since your lifetime capital gains exclusion of $125,000 (on a sale of the home) cannot be applied against the children's remainder interest.

To Illustrate

Fred, age sixty-eight, transfers his home to his son, Dave, but reserves a life estate. Two years after the transfer Fred and Dave agree to sell the home, since Fred intends to move in with Dave. The home cost $50,000 and is to be sold for $250,000. The value of Fred's share (his life estate) in the property is about 60 percent and therefore Dave's share is about 40 percent. Accordingly, Fred's gain will be 60 percent × $200,000, or $120,000 on which he will pay no taxes because of the over-fifty-five exclusion, and Dave's gain will be 40 percent of $200,000, or $80,000 on which he will pay a tax of about $24,000.

If, for some reason, all of you did agree that the home should be sold, this would pose no legal problem, because the buyer would purchase both your rights to live there and your children's underlying rights to ownership. These are the rights we normally get when we purchase a home. Aside from the possible capital gains tax problem, such a sale is far less complicated than it sounds. Your life estate would continue in the proceeds of the sale, meaning that you would have the right to the income (and in certain cases part of the principal) from the sale proceeds for your life. On your death the remaining principal would belong to the children.

As a planning alternative, you could split the proceeds into two shares, one for the present value of the life estate and the other for the present value of the remainder. Then you could apply planning strategies to your share.

Tip ——————————————————————————————

> As mentioned earlier, the sale of a home under a reserved life estate is generally a bad idea. It can affect Medicaid eligibility and, as noted previously, generate an unexpected (and otherwise avoidable) capital gains tax to the children. It should be considered only where there is no other option.

If there was a sale of your home, and if all or part of the proceeds from the sale were used to purchase another house, you and your spouse would have a life estate in the *new* house, stemming from your original gift with a reserved life estate, though the children would still have to pay a capital gains tax on their share of the gain on the sale of the original house; they could not "roll over" their gain to the new house.

Tip

If there *is* a sale and a purchase of a new home, *be sure* the deed to the new home reflects your life estate. Otherwise, you would be considered to have made another gift (the value of the life estate), which could disqualify you for Medicaid benefits.

While you occupied the home (as a "life tenant"), you would pay no "rent," although you would be responsible for normal maintenance expenses (but not capital improvements or major repairs). Unless otherwise agreed, you would also have to pay the real estate taxes, which would be deductible to you. The children would be responsible for the major items, as well as insurance, unless you reached some other agreement with them.

Tip

Be sure your attorney knows the proper language to use in drafting a deed with a reserved life estate. Use of the wrong wording can cause serious problems.

To Illustrate

Some attorneys describe the life estate only in terms of the right to occupy (as opposed to the right to rents, use, etc.) and go on to say that if the person ceases to occupy the property, on account of institutionalization for example, then the "life estate" terminates. The problem with this language is that such an event (institutionalization) would effectively cause a potentially disqualifying transfer since the person would be losing or involuntarily transferring the value of his life estate (due to his automatic loss of the right of occupancy). Thus, the wrong choice of words could be disastrous not only from a Medicaid standpoint but from a capital gains tax standpoint as illustrated above.

As with any transaction, there are some risks to consider, but in this case they are not, in my opinion, prohibitive. For instance, there are the risks that one of your children could be sued or become involved in a divorce or die. In any of these cases, the child's rights of ownership would be reachable by the child's spouse or creditor, but, as noted, you would still have your life estate, uninterrupted. In the case of a child's death, the value of his or her remainder interest would be included in the child's estate, but this would not interfere with your occupancy. *In every case, your right to live in the home for your lifetime would not be disrupted.*

If after making a gift of the home and reserving a joint life estate, you or your spouse entered a nursing home, the other would, of course, have the right to remain in the residence. Even if both of you entered a nursing home, or if the survivor did, your right to live in your home remains intact. A life estate means for life, unless the life tenant releases the life estate on his or her own. If neither life tenant is able to occupy the property because they are both institutionalized, the property could (or may have to) be rented, and the rents, after expenses, would have to be applied toward the care of one or both parties, but this is a small price to pay for preservation of the entire home.

To Illustrate

> About two years after Max and Ellen deeded their home to their children, reserving life estates for themselves, Ellen died. Then, a few months after that, Max had to enter a nursing home. The children left Max's home vacant until it became clear that Max would never return. In the meanwhile, Max had been declared eligible for Medicaid benefits. The children decided to rent the home and found a tenant for $900 per month. After an allowance for taxes, expenses, and insurance, this left a "profit" of about $500 per month, which would have to be paid toward Max's care. Further, the rents and expenses are generally reviewed every six months by the Medicaid agency (while Max is on Medicaid) to determine whether any adjustments should be made in the amount that must be paid toward Max's care. The home itself, however, is *protected* from reach by the state, because Max does not own it — he has only the right to *live* there. Note: In some states, the remaining value of Max's life estate, measured the moment before his death, may be subject to estate recovery (see Chapter 8).

Getting back to the gift, the value of your gift (of the remainder interest), for purposes of the federal gift tax, would be the fair market value of the home at the time of the gift, *less* the value of your respective life estate. The IRS has tables for this purpose, so the value of your right to live in the house can be readily ascertained in most cases.

And, as noted earlier, you should not worry about paying any gift tax unless the value of the gift exceeds $600,000. (Actually, it could be *double* this amount in some cases, but that's beyond the scope of this discussion.)

Important Note

The value of the gift also would be reduced by any mortgage, but if there is a mortgage, a gift of the house would probably cause the bank to call for payment in full. Furthermore, there could be adverse tax implications with a mortgage. For these reasons, this type of gift is normally done only where there is no outstanding mortgage.

Important Reminder

Unless the gift of the remainder interest falls under one of the four exceptions listed in Chapter 3, the transfer of the home with a reserved life estate will trigger the thirty-six-month waiting period for Medicaid purposes.

Nevertheless, if all indications are that you should use a gift with a reserved life estate, the results can be that:
• You would be protecting your right to live in the property for your life (or if spouses, for both of your lives).
• For Medicaid purposes the home would be protected from countability, at least after the thirty-six-month period following the tax.
• On the death of the life tenant(s), the property would avoid probate, saving considerable legal fees and in some states, exposure to claims, probably including Medicaid liens on the property (but see my discussion on this in Chapter 8).
• There would be no gift tax on the transfer.

- Your children would ultimately receive the home with a stepped-up cost basis, thereby materially reducing or possibly even eliminating any capital gains tax on their later sale of the home after your death.

Disadvantages to a gift of the home reserving a life estate are (1) that a sale of the home during your lifetime(s) will likely generate a capital gains tax to the children (or other remaindermen), and (2) that you have given up control over the final disposition of your home. Although in some cases the family situation is clear enough so that an irrevocable gift is indicated, no one can positively foretell the future. If you have any reservation about this loss of control (even though you know you will have the uninterrupted right to live in the home), you may instead consider transferring the home to a revocable trust.

Placing the Home in a Trust

Most if not all of the advantages of a gift with a reserved life estate result from placing the home in a trust, but it is a little more complicated and has become *far less desirable* after the late 1993 changes to the Medicaid laws. From a legal standpoint, this option is somewhat more expensive (though by no means prohibitive), since your attorney must draft a trust instrument. The next question to consider is whether the trust is to be *revocable* (changeable at any time by you) or *irrevocable* (unchangeable).

Obviously, there are many more legal considerations involved in choosing an irrevocable trust (as opposed to a revocable trust), not the least of which is the loss of control *and* the triggering of the longer, *sixty*-month waiting period under the Medicaid laws, since a transfer to an irrevocable trust is unlikely to fall under any of the exceptions to the Medicaid rules. And, depending on the provisions of the irrevocable trust, if you transfer your home to such a trust, you also will be converting the home (a noncountable asset) into a countable asset because you no longer own the home and cannot get it back. Instead, you would now own a beneficial interest in an irrevocable trust that owns the home.

By far the simpler option is to transfer the home to a *revoca-*

ble trust. Because a revocable trust gives you the right to take back the home at any time or to do anything else you wish with it, *a transfer of the home to a revocable trust is not a transfer as contemplated by the Medicaid laws and therefore would not trigger the thirty-six-month Medicaid waiting period.* However, if the owner/transferor is institutionalized, the government treats this transfer as a *conversion* of the home from a noncountable asset to a *countable* asset, so there is no benefit to the transfer. Therefore, for Medicaid purposes there are no longer any advantages to transferring the home to a revocable trust.

Tip

> For these reasons, it is only in rare cases that it will be helpful or advisable to transfer your home into a trust. The rare case could include, for instance, a single individual who wants to keep complete control of the house through the irrevocable trust and is willing and able to wait up to sixty months before eligibility instead of the thirty-six months applicable to non-trust transfers.

Important Note

> Since you keep control of the property through your trust (or even if you give up control but keep certain benefits, such as the right to live in the home), there will be no estate or income tax savings in creating such a trust. This is not a problem, however, since the issue here is protection and preservation of the home, and not tax savings. (See more coverage of this later.)

What to Do with an Out-of-State Home

Out-of-state homes give rise to a special problem where Medicaid planning is concerned. That is, when a person from one state decides to enter a nursing home in another state and apply for Medicaid there, he must declare himself a principal resident of the latter state. If he is a principal resident of one state, he cannot at the same time have principal residence in another state. Therefore, if he has a "home" in another state, it will immediately become a countable asset since it can no longer be classified as his home, and he will *not* qualify for Medicaid in the second state. Accordingly, the out-of-state home will have to be sold, and some or all of the proceeds used toward nursing home costs, depriving the family of the funds.

In a situation like this, it is imperative to take steps *before* the individual moves to another state. While he still has his residence in the first state, he should consider transferring the residence before the move. If at all possible, a transfer should be made which will not violate the Medicaid rules (to a spouse, for instance). In any event, the law of the foreign state should be examined to determine just what transfers of the home are allowable. (See Case Study 3 in Chapter 11 for an illustration.)

To Illustrate

> Harry and Sally have their home in Florida and intend to move to Massachusetts to be with their children. Harry is not well and is likely to enter a nursing home in the near future. If they keep their Florida home after the move, it will be a fully countable asset for Medicaid purposes. They could sell the Florida residence and purchase a Massachusetts residence in *Sally's* name, and the new home would then be an exempt asset. After Harry qualifies for Medicaid, Sally can sell or transfer the new home without affecting Harry's Medicaid benefits.

If the person is already in the new state, it may be advisable to consider moving back to the state of his residence until the home can be properly transferred without jeopardizing his Medicaid benefits. In the "worst-case condition," where none of the above options is possible, the out-of-state home will have to be sold, but the sales proceeds in excess of thirty-six months of projected nursing home costs could be gifted away so that they may be protected.

Use of Trusts

How a Trust Works

A trust is a legal arrangement in which one person, called the *settlor* (or donor, or grantor), transfers some type of property to another party, called the *trustee,* to hold and manage for the benefit of one or more other individuals, called the *beneficiaries*. (Note that the settlor of the trust can also be the trustee, *as well as* a beneficiary, so long as there is another designated beneficiary after the settlor's death.)

From its simplest form to its most complex, every trust is based upon the same principle and contains the same basic elements: a donor, a trustee, some property, and one or more beneficiaries.

Any trust you create while you are alive is called a *living* trust. A trust created under your will (and therefore at your death) is called a *testamentary* trust. Under many trusts, the donor will reserve the right to "alter, amend, or revoke" the trust. This simply means he can do whatever he pleases with the trust or with any property held in the trust. The retention of a right to change or revoke the trust — called a *revocable* trust — does *not* provide the donor with any immediate tax or Medicaid benefits but *will* allow the property in the trust to avoid the costs, delays, and publicity of probate on the donor's disability or death.

The opposite of a revocable trust is an irrevocable trust. *If a trust does not specifically contain the right of the donor to amend or revoke the trust, it is automatically irrevocable, and it generally cannot be changed.*

Whether your trust is living or testamentary, whether it is revocable or irrevocable, and whether it is a simple "trustee" bank account or a complicated Medicaid trust, once it takes effect it will work the same way.

When property is transferred to the trustee, the trustee immediately begins to manage, maintain, or invest the trust property, whether it be cash, securities, real estate, or other property, according to the instructions given by the donor (normally contained in the written trust document).

To Illustrate

Say that John gives $1,000 to Adrienne with instructions that she give him all the interest it earns, and that on John's death, she should turn the balance over to John's sister Adele. Adrienne's duties are quite clear. She will pay John all the interest on the $1,000 up to his death, and then she will transfer the remaining funds over to Adele, directly. Adele then owns the money outright and Adrienne's job as trustee is completed.

Of course, the instructions and the duties could be much more involved. John could have transferred real estate to Adrienne, or a large portfolio of various securities, and Adrienne would then have been responsible for the proper management of the trust property. This might include renting the property, keeping it properly insured and in good repair, and so on. If she were holding securities, she would be responsible for keeping track of the progress of the various companies whose stock she was holding, or she might simply hire an investment advisor. For doing all of this, she is entitled to a reasonable trustee fee. In any event, once the property is transferred to the trust, the trustee's responsibility is to care for it while carrying out the donor's instructions to her.

Creating the trust, however, is only half the battle. If you want it to do anything for you, it has to be *funded.* This means actually transferring title to your assets into the name of the trust. Otherwise, it could prove useless.

As illustrated above, assets that are transferred to your trust will be managed and distributed according to the terms of the trust. In most instances, this means that the assets will avoid probate on your legal disability and on your death.

Medicaid trusts follow all of these basic rules, and, once funded, they work like any other trust, *except* that in order to protect assets, they must contain some very special provisions, which are described later. But first, it might help to understand how and why so-called Medicaid trusts came about.

Background on Medicaid Trusts

Concern over impoverishment on account of long term care costs is not new. For many years people have entered into various arrangements designed to protect their assets, focusing primarily on their savings and investments, since the home has for some time been given "exempt" status. Sometime around the early- to mid-1970s, a plan surfaced proposing that a person could create a certain form of trust that would give him the complete use and enjoyment of his savings and investments, yet at the same time protect these assets from Medicaid, allowing the person to qualify for Medicaid benefits if he had to enter a nursing home. For obvious reasons, the idea caught on, and tens of thousands of families created such trusts.

In the typical case, the applicant would create an irrevocable, "fully discretionary" trust and transfer most or all of his savings and investments to that trust. A child or other trusted individual would be the trustee and would be given the authority to distribute to the applicant or his spouse *any* income or principal that he, the trustee, decided to give, *in his discretion* (hence the term "fully discretionary trust"). Since the applicant had given up control over the assets and since, legally, he could not force the trustee to exercise his discretion, the assets in the trust were considered "inaccessible" to the applicant, and, as discussed earlier, inaccessible assets are not countable for Medicaid purposes. As a result, even though a person had several hundred thousand dollars in an irrevocable, fully discretionary trust, he could nevertheless qualify for Medicaid benefits, since the trust funds were not accessible to him.

To stop this "abuse," the federal government enacted, as part of the 1986 COBRA (Consolidated Omnibus Budget Reconciliation Act) law, a new rule providing that the assets in a trust would be *fully countable* to the extent that the trustee has discretion to distribute them, *whether or not* the trustee exercised his discretion, if the trust was created (and funded) by the Medicaid applicant (or beneficiary) or by the applicant's spouse.

What this meant was that *all* the assets in a fully discretionary trust (*regardless* of when the trust was created) would be counted as available to the individual beneficiary if he *or* his spouse created (and funded) the trust during his or her lifetime. All states have subsequently adopted similar regulations. Therefore, for both federal and state purposes, virtually all trusts of this sort were affected, even those discretionary irrevocable trusts created *before* the change in the law.

If you or someone in your family has an irrevocable discretionary trust created before the COBRA change, you should seek immediate legal counsel to see if any relief can be obtained. For instance, if the trust allows the trustee to make distributions of principal to someone other than the Medicaid candidate, such a distribution should be considered because it would not be treated as a transfer by the Medicaid applicant. An examination of the trust may reveal other possibilities. In the worst case (where the Medicaid candidate was the sole beneficiary during his lifetime), all of the principal could be distributed to the Medicaid candidate, who in turn could make gifts, purchase exempt assets, or create a new trust that would not violate the COBRA rules. Unfortunately, this will require a new waiting period, so be sure to set aside enough to cover the costs for this period.

An exception to both the federal and state COBRA changes exists for trusts funded under a will. In other words, if a husband's will provided that assets would pass from his *probate* estate into a trust for the benefit of his wife, then the assets in that trust (to the extent received from the deceased husband's *probate* estate) would not be countable for purposes of his wife's eligibility for Medicaid. This would be so *even though* the trust was a fully discretionary trust, which, if funded with these assets during the husband's lifetime, would have been otherwise countable.

To Illustrate

John is extremely ill and not expected to live more than eighteen months or so. Mary, his wife, is elderly and in frail condition. Though it is not imminent, there are serious concerns that Mary will have to enter a nursing home in the future. John and Mary's assets consist of a home and about $280,000 in savings, all in joint names.

Mary transfers her share of the home as well as the savings into John's name alone. John's attorney prepares a new will for John, and the will contains a *testamentary* trust for

Mary's benefit. The trustee, John's son, may make payments to Mary at his discretion. On Mary's death, the balance in the trust passes to John and Mary's children.

When John dies, the discretionary trust will be funded through his probate estate and all the savings plus the home will be protected. If they had done nothing and Mary became the sole owner of all the assets, it is likely that everything would have been lost.

Important Note

For the most part, planning for this exception applies only in very specific cases. For instance, where one spouse is terminally ill and the other may enter a nursing home, it may be advisable to cause assets to pass through the terminally ill spouse's probate estate to fund a discretionary trust for the benefit of the other spouse.

As usually happens, every time the government passes a law curtailing some "abuse," lawyers and other advisors immediately set their planning minds to work to develop strategies that comply with the new law. The OBRA Medicaid trust law was no exception. It became an accepted strategy to create a trust which provided discretionary payments for the first thirty months (the applicable waiting period at that time), then limit payments to *income* (not principal). Thus, after only a thirty-month wait, the principal was protected. Then along came OBRA 1993.

Once again, to stem the "abuses" of Medicaid planning, Congress aimed to make it more difficult and inconvenient to use trusts for this purpose. And they succeeded, though they did not, by any means, make it impossible. Although the laws are extremely complicated and poorly written, it is clear that certain types of trusts can still be used to protect assets — the problem, for the most part, will be the increased waiting period.

Basically, if a trust is to be effective in protecting a person's assets, the person must not, *under any circumstances,* have the opportunity to receive payments of principal from the trust. In other words, discretionary trusts established by the individual or his spouse are out (with the exception of the testamentary trust explained earlier). Furthermore, transfers to this type of trust will be subject to a sixty-month wait before the individual (or his spouse) can be eligible for Medicaid. Unless your state has adopted a later date, *THESE RULES WILL APPLY TO TRUSTS ESTABLISHED AFTER AUGUST 10, 1993.*

OBRA 1993 added other trust options that could be helpful in certain cases. These options were presented as exceptions to the above rules under certain circumstances. These two exceptions have come to be known as the "under-sixty-five trust" and the "pooled trust." Both exceptions apply only to "disabled" individuals as defined in the Social Security laws and both exceptions require the state to be repaid, to the extent possible, from the funds remaining in the trust on the Medicaid beneficiary's death. The amount of repayment would be equal to the Medicaid benefits the state paid on behalf of the individual.

Under-Sixty-five Trusts

If a trust which meets the necessary qualifications is established for a permanently disabled individual who is under the age of sixty-five, the assets of the trust will *not* be counted for Medicaid purposes, nor will the transfer to the trust be subject to any waiting period. Though this may appear attractive, the requirements are strict:

• The trust must be established by the parent, grandparent, or legal guardian of the individual, or by a court. It may not be established by the individual himself or by his spouse.

• The trust must be "for the sole benefit of" the individual. That is, no one other than the individual may be able to receive benefits from the trust during the individual's lifetime nor after the individual's death until the state is fully reimbursed for all Medicaid benefits paid to the individual.

• No additions may be made to the trust after the individual reaches age sixty-five.

Although the trust may appear to be of limited benefit because of the requirement that the state be reimbursed on the death of the individual, there may be opportunities for savings in the difference between the amount that the state pays for Medicaid benefits versus the private pay cost. The accumulated savings of this difference over the year could end up benefiting the family.

Pooled Trusts

The second exception is the *pooled trust*. This trust may benefit disabled individuals of any age but it must be established by a nonprofit association, presumably to benefit any number of qualifying individuals for whose benefit contributions are made to the trust. Because of this pooling nature, the law requires that separate *"accounts"* be established "for the sole benefit of" qualifying individuals. Like the under-sixty-five trust, the accounts may be established by the parent, grandparent, or legal guardian of the individual, or by a court, but unlike the under-sixty-five trust, the pooled trust may also be established by the individual himself.

Contributions to the pooled trust are not exempt from the transfer rules, so the individual will have to wait a period of time before Medicaid eligibility. However, once eligibility is established, the assets in the trust will not be counted as resources. Like the under-sixty-five trust, the state must be reimbursed from the pooled trust on the individual's death for benefits paid. Any amounts left may continue to be held in trust or paid to the individual's beneficiaries.

Miller Trusts

There is a third exception to the trust rule, though it is only applicable in certain states. As discussed in Chapter 1, some states (called "income cap" states) place a *limit* on the amount of income a person can have and qualify for Medicaid. If income exceeds that limit, even by a dollar, the person cannot qualify.

In recognition of the ridiculous results this arrangement can produce (e.g., where an incompetent disabled person is institutionalized, has absolutely no assets and only income which is just over the "cap"), OBRA allows a trust to be established for such individuals, funded with the income that the person would have otherwise received. (These are called "Miller" trusts, after the name of a case dealing with the problem.) If the Miller trust meets the requirements, the person can qualify for Medicaid in the income cap state, even though his income exceeds the cap.

This is done by "assigning" or paying to the trust all of the income (Social Security, pension, etc.) due to the individual. If the trust provides that the income is to be used for payment of the individual's care (or for the individual's spouse), then there will be no transfer of assets penalty upon placing the income into the trust.

Revocable Trusts

This type of trust, which is fully controllable and revocable by the person who created it (the "settlor"), generally offers *no* advantage in qualifying for Medicaid benefits, because the settlor/applicant has full access to the assets in the trust. Furthermore, the Medicaid rules provide that transfers to third parties (someone other than the applicant or his spouse) out of *revocable* trusts will be subject to the *sixty*-month penalty period.

Irrevocable Trusts

Unless one of the special exceptions discussed above applies, the typical family is left only one option if a trust is desired: an irrevocable income-only trust, which is likely to involve a waiting period of sixty months, depending on the amount transferred to the trust. As noted, the spouses can have *no* rights to principal, although the trust could allow principal payments to be made to others, such as children. Even though this sounds strict, as a practical matter most elderly couples make a great effort to use only the income from their investments and avoid touching the principal. If this is the case, the income-only trust can be worthwhile.

To Illustrate _____

John and Mary have accumulated savings and investments of about $350,000, resulting from the recent sale of their home. They currently live off the income but are concerned that if either of them becomes ill and requires long term care, their funds will be quickly dissipated. They create an irrevocable trust to which they transfer all of these assets. The trust provides that all the income (but *only* the income) will be paid to the two of them for their lives, provided that if either enters a nursing home, the income will then be paid to the *healthy* spouse for life, then all the income to the survivor for life, and on the death of both, the trust will terminate and the balance in the trust will be paid over to their children. During their lives they would have *no* access to the principal of the trust. Under these provisions John and Mary's assets should be *fully protected* for Medicaid purposes approximately sixty months after they make the transfer to the trust.

Furthermore, in the example above only half the income would be counted for either spouse until he or she entered the nursing home, and then *all* of the income would be protected for the healthy spouse. About the only drawback is the wait, and also, as stated above, the fact that neither John nor Mary would have any access to the principal of their trust. To add additional flexibility, therefore, it is possible to give the trustee of their trust the power to make distributions of trust principal to the "issue" (lineal descendants) of John and Mary. This would mean that the trustee (*other than* John or Mary) could make occasional lump-sum payments of principal to John and Mary's children and/or grandchildren. In addition to flexibility, this option adds a sort of "safety valve" to the trust, so that if there is a drastic change in the law or the family circumstances, the trust could legally be dissolved (by the trustee's distribution of all the principal) if dissolution was in the best interest of the family.

Important Note

When a trust such as the one described in the above example is used and the sixty-month wait applies, *no further penalty period* occurs if payments of principal are later made to children or grandchildren from the trust. Therefore, payments by the trustee to beneficiaries other than the applicant or his spouse will *not* incur a penalty.

To Illustrate

Joseph, a widower, places $200,000 into an irrevocable trust that pays him only the income from the trust assets for the rest of his life. The trust also provides that Joseph's son, Able, has the right to direct payment out of the trust for all or any part of the trust principal to any of Joseph's lineal descendants except to Able himself.

Two years later, it becomes desirable to withdraw $80,000 for Able's daughter, Alice. Able simply directs the trustee to pay that amount to Alice from the trust principal. Since the only irrevocable transfer that *Joseph* made was the initial $200,000 contribution to the trust, the subsequent payment of $80,000 directed by Able from the already transferred $200,000 will not constitute another transfer by Joseph. However, the waiting period resulting from the initial $200,000 transfer will not be changed.

Tip

If you use this alternative approach, you should provide for a second person to exercise the special power to direct principal in case the first one named becomes incompetent or dies. This precaution is not necessary with the first suggestion (payment directed by the trustee) because a trust must have a trustee.

One problem with the income-only trust described above and the triggering of the waiting period as a result of the transfer to the trust is that if the grantor or his spouse had to enter a nursing home *within* the waiting period, they would not have access to any funds to pay for the ill spouse's care. And since Medicaid would not pay, it could create a family crisis. To avoid this problem, I suggest leaving a certain amount of funds *outside* the trust to be used for this purpose. As another (in many cases, more desirable) second alternative, if possible, purchase nursing home insurance to cover the individual during the waiting period.

Warning

You may have noted that the Medicaid law restricting discretionary trusts applies only to trusts created by the applicant/settlor or his spouse. In other words, if someone *else*, say a child, creates a discretionary trust for you or your spouse, then the assets in that trust would apparently not be countable for Medicaid purposes. Using this exception as an incentive, some of the more aggressive advisors have therefore suggested the following scenario: John and his wife, Mary, make a gift of the $250,000 in savings to their two children. A while later, the children, in apparent appreciation of the largesse of their parents, create a fully discretionary irrevocable trust to the benefit of their parents, funding it with around $250,000. In my opinion, this spells trouble with a capital T, and perhaps even raises the question of fraud. I would not recommend it. Further, OBRA contains specific provisions prohibiting the arrangement.

Tip

If your attorney suggests this approach, and if you decide to go along with it despite the obvious risks, I suggest that your "children's" trust contain some form of safety valve that will allow some means of terminating the trust, so that you can start over when the state tells you that all of the assets in your fully discretionary trust are going to be counted for Medicaid purposes.

Remember, creating an irrevocable trust that you cannot control and transferring all your savings and investments to it while you are still healthy is a drastic move. It should never be done without careful deliberation *and* expert counsel. In the past, those who were not quite ready to give up control but still wanted to protect their assets in the event of a catastrophic illness would instead consider a "convertible" trust. As noted, however, the convertible trust is likely to become "a thing of the past."

Convertible Trusts

The convertible trust illustrates the flexibility offered by a trust. In effect, it shows that a trust can be tailored and fine-tuned to cover almost any conceivable situation. The convertible trust is designed to be fully controllable and revocable by the settlor while he is alive and well, but *upon his institutionalization it automatically becomes irrevocable,* with the objective of providing for the settlor and his spouse while protecting the family assets.

In this case, we would start with a relatively standard revocable trust, to which the settlor transfers his savings and investments. The trust contains another very important provision, however, stating that at such time as the settlor or his spouse becomes a permanent resident of a nursing home or similar long term care facility (the trust would clearly specify how this event would be determined — usually by a physician's statement), the trust would thereupon become irrevocable, and both the settlor and his spouse would be entitled to receive *only the income* from the trust. During the waiting period, however, which would begin at the time the trust became irrevocable, the settlor and his spouse would also be entitled to *principal* distributions for the reasons discussed above. However, OBRA now provides that the waiting period will not begin until the individual and his spouse have absolutely no rights to principal. So a convertible trust could leave you shortchanged for up to a *sixty-month* period. (If the trust income were high enough, it might be possible to dispense with the principal distributions to the spouses altogether.) If the settlor (or his spouse) never suffers a catastrophic illness requiring institutionalization, the trust *remains* revocable by the settlor until his death.

Important Note

> Do not be tempted to use "form-book" trusts or books with tear-out, fill-in-the-blank forms, Medicaid or otherwise. Some people look to these as a means of saving legal fees. It never ceases to amaze me how a person will risk the safety and protection of his home and his entire life's savings on such forms without the benefit of expert counsel, just to save legal fees. Believe me, it is never worth it, and more often than not, you'll end up paying more, most of it to lawyers!

Comments on Various Trust Provisions

Lawyers are often criticized for using "standard" forms and charging clients high prices for an "off-the-shelf" item. What clients don't seem to understand is that the wrong off-the-shelf item, the inclusion of the wrong provision, or the omission of the right one in a "standard" trust can prove almost as catastrophic as the illnesses we have been talking about.

A competent attorney will realize that a special situation — such as Medicaid planning — requires a careful review and constant updating of all standard provisions as well as the inclusion of some new provisions to ensure that the client's objectives will be met to the extent possible under the law. In fact, it may well be that your present attorney will refer you to another who is more expert in the now specialized field of Medicaid planning.

In any event, here are some simple observations for you and your attorney to consider with respect to the "usual" provisions of a Medicaid trust:

Selection of Trustees

In the fully discretionary trusts that were created prior to the 1986 COBRA law, it was necessary to appoint a trustee other than the settlor or his spouse, since they were also the discretionary beneficiaries. If a trustee was also a discretionary beneficiary, this could be interpreted for Medicaid purposes as having no trust at all, since the trustee had discretion to pay all the trust funds to himself. With an income-only trust, however, or any type of Medicaid trust where the trustee is restricted in making payments, it does not matter who is trustee, so long as he or she is competent to perform the functions of the trustee.

In the typical Medicaid type of trust, the settlor (and/or his spouse) would be the initial trustee; then, if for any reason he ceased to serve, his spouse and then perhaps a child could succeed him. If larger amounts of money or investments are involved, or if there is no logical family member to serve, you should consider a professional trustee, such as a bank or trust company. As a general rule, I do not recommend naming your lawyer or accountant as trustee unless you have a long-term, proven relationship with her, and you are sure she will have the time to attend to the proper administration of your trust. Finally, if you do name anyone other than a spouse as trustee, you should consider giving the spouse and/or your children the power to remove the trustee and appoint a successor, just in case problems arise in the future.

Selection of Beneficiaries

Normally, you and your spouse, if any, will be the only beneficiaries while you are alive (except for those trusts that provide for discretionary distributions of principal to children or grandchildren as a safety valve). When both you and your spouse are deceased, the children, if any, would receive the balance of the trust funds. However, depending upon your family situation, you may get a little more sophisticated here and provide for children, grandchildren, or other "charities" on your death. It is important to review this thoroughly with your lawyer. In any event, do not, as stated earlier, make your "estate" the beneficiary of your trust, unless it is one of those situations involving the need for a testamentary trust discussed above.

Court-Approved Provisions

Whenever possible, avoid any provisions in your trust that require approval or action by a "court of proper jurisdiction" or any similar language requiring court action. All this does is involve the trust and the beneficiaries with the probate court and its attendant legal fees, delays, and publicity, which in most cases can be easily avoided if the trust is properly drafted.

Safety Valves

As discussed above, it's a good idea to have some means of either distributing principal out of the trust or terminating the trust should the law or the family circumstances materially change. One way to do this is to give someone, say a child, or in other cases, the trustee (other than you or your spouse), the power to distribute principal among a specified group — that is, children and/or grandchildren, but not to you or your spouse.

Important Note _____

> Some advisors feel that a provision can be included stating that if the existence of the trust causes a disqualification of the grantors from receiving Medicaid benefits, then the trust will thereupon terminate and the balance be paid over to the children or other beneficiaries. It is very clear in the law that such a provision offers *no* protection whatever, *so leave it out!*

Protecting Assets Through a Spouse's Right to Income

As discussed in Chapter 2, once a spouse is institutionalized and determined to be eligible for Medicaid benefits, the healthy spouse is at the same time permitted to receive a monthly income allowance based on federal poverty guidelines, up to a maximum monthly income allowance of $1,500 (adjusted annually for inflation — the 1995 amount was $1,870).

Also remember that the healthy spouse is separately permitted to keep the spousal *resource* allowance, also discussed in Chapter 2, up to a maximum allowance of $60,000 (adjusted annually for inflation — the 1995 amount was $74,820).

Fortunately, both "maximum" allowances are subject to exceptions, and, through one of these exceptions, the income allowance can bring about a higher *resource* allowance, thereby preserving additional assets for the healthy spouse.

If the healthy spouse can show that the spousal resource allowance granted her by the state does not produce income that, together with all her other income, equals her specified monthly income allowance, the state, on a request for a fair hearing by the healthy spouse, must increase the spousal resource in an amount sufficient to produce income equal to the monthly income allowance.

Special Note

As of this writing, several states have been disputing this rule and interpreting the federal rule to mean that if the at-home spouse's income is under the income allowance, then, instead of increasing the resource allowance, the state may first apply the institutionalized spouse's income to make up the difference. There has been a great deal of dispute over this "income first" rule, and in at least one case (the Ohio case of *Kimnach v. Ohio Dept. of Human Services,* 9/8/94), the state *lost.* Nevertheless, most practitioners are fairly certain that the federal law requires the states to increase the Resource Allowance, so spouses whose income is less than the income allowance have no choice but to appeal.

To Illustrate

John and Mary have a home and countable assets worth $200,000. The assets are invested in a certificate of deposit (CD) earning 5 percent interest, for a total of $10,000 per year income. Mary's only other income is Social Security of $400 per month. John enters a nursing home, and a determination is made that Mary will be permitted to keep a spousal resource allowance of $74,820 plus a monthly income allowance of $1,500. Since Mary will have her own income of $400 from Social Security, plus an additional $312 per month interest from her $74,820 spousal resource allowance, which is generated by the 5 percent CD ($74,820 × 5 percent/12 months = about $312 per month), she should be allowed an additional $788 per month from John's income to bring her income up to the $1,500 per month allowance. However, John's income (without the CD) is only $400 per month from a generous state pension. This can also go to Mary, but the total ($312 + $400 + $400 = $1,112) still leaves Mary $388 per month short of the $1,500 monthly income allowance. Mary must request a fair hearing (see Chapter 9 for discussion on this), asking that her spousal resource allowance be increased to generate additional income sufficient to meet her monthly income allowance. In this case, using the 5 percent CD as a measure of investment rates, the state should allow Mary an additional $93,120 which, at 5 percent, would generate the needed additional income of $388 per month.

Presumably, once this increase in the resource allowance is granted, the money (or other assets) becomes Mary's and she may do with it as she pleases. However, several states are taking the position that the shortfall of income should be made up by the purchase of an *annuity* for the life of the at-home spouse, which will pay to the spouse a monthly income equal to the shortfall. And this option is given only if there is still a shortfall after application of the "income first" rule as discussed above.

The result is to disregard Congress's intent to provide an adequate income to the at-home spouse, because under this approach on the death of the institutionalized spouse, the at-home spouse will lose the income from the institutionalized spouse without the ability to replace it. Hopefully, the courts and states will soon recognize this inequity and grant the at-home spouse a greater resource allowance, without conditions attached.*

Even if the increase in the spousal resource allowance is given without conditions, it would *NOT* automatically mean that Mary can give away the increased amount and then seek another increase because she no longer has adequate income. Once the income and resource allowances are established, it is unlikely that a change in Mary's circumstances will warrant a redetermination, although the law is unclear on the point. (It is also the case that if Mary makes a transfer of all or any of her spousal resource allowance before John qualifies for Medicaid, it will be treated as a disqualifying transfer.)

In summary, if at the time of approval of Medicaid benefits for the institutionalized spouse or at the time the income allowance is established, the healthy spouse can show that the assets she is allowed to keep do not generate income that, together with her other income, equals the monthly income allowance established for her by

* Courts in Ohio (1994) and Massachusetts (1995) have declared that the income first rule is a violation of federal law.

the state, then she can ask for additional family assets sufficient to generate the extra income. This can be accomplished by requesting a fair hearing, as explained in Chapter 9.

Somewhat akin to this approach to an increase in the spousal resource allowance is a court order for an institutionalized spouse to pay monthly support to a healthy spouse. (This is discussed in more detail later.)

Tip _____

After the spousal resource and income allowances are determined, the healthy spouse should be careful to continue to keep her income and accounts separate from those of the institutionalized spouse to avoid accumulating future funds in his name.

Important Note _____

A critical fact that many seem to overlook is that at the end of any given month, income for that month not disposed of becomes *principal* in the next month. If the institutionalized spouse on Medicaid accumulates more than $2,000 of principal, he could be disqualified from Medicaid, until the excess is spent down for his care. Make sure that this does not happen.

It should also be kept in mind that for most families, tax planning is secondary to Medicaid planning for preservation of assets. Nevertheless, it is important to understand the basic tax ramifications of the various Medicaid strategies, as they may make a difference in your choice of options. Therefore, in the following pages I explain the tax rules that apply to your plan.

What Are the Tax Effects of Gifts, Life Estates, and Trusts?

The following tax discussion, unless otherwise noted, generally reflects the effect on transfers to a person other than a spouse. For federal *gift tax* purposes, spouses (who are US citizens) may freely make unlimited gifts to each other with no gift tax consequences. Most states have no gift taxes at all. For federal and state *income tax* purposes, there will be no shifting of income on gifts between spouses if the spouses file a joint income tax return, as most do. For federal *estate tax* purposes, property left to a surviving spouse (who is a US citizen) enjoys an unlimited marital deduction, so there will be no federal estate tax on amounts left to the surviving spouse.

Gifts

Where an outright gift is made and you have totally separated yourself from ownership, control, and benefits of the gifted property, the following tax results will normally occur:

Income taxes: You will no longer be taxed on any income produced by the gift, beginning with income earned on the gifted property from and after the date of the gift. The donee of the gift assumes your cost basis on the gifted property for purposes of capital gains tax on a later sale.

Gift taxes: If the value of the gifted property on the date of the gift exceeds $600,000 (after subtracting the annual $10,000 per donee exclusions, where they apply) and you have no spouse, you will owe a federal gift tax. If you have made taxable gifts (over $10,000 per person per year) in the past, they will be added back as part of the $600,000. (Check Appendix B to see if there may be a state gift tax that applies.) For instance, John, a widower, made a gift of $80,000 to his daughter in 1990. After subtracting the $10,000 exclusion, this left $70,000, which would be applied toward John's $600,000 lifetime exemption. If John were to make a gift to his daughter in 1992 that exceeded $540,000 ($530,000 remaining lifetime exemption plus the $10,000 annual exclusion for 1992), then he would owe a federal gift tax on the excess.

Estate taxes: If the gift exceeds $10,000 to any person in a given year, the federal law requires that all such excesses be added back to your estate (for tax computation purposes only). However, each estate is entitled to the equivalent of a $600,000 exemption, and, therefore, federal estate taxes will not, for most Medicaid cases, be a consideration.

Gifts with a Reserved Life Estate

Income taxes: Since you have reserved the income or possibly other benefits from this gift, the tax laws, both federal and state, provide that you will be taxed on all the income from the property, if any. Similarly, you will be entitled to deduct any annual loss. If the gift was your home and you paid the real estate taxes, you may deduct them. If the home is sold, however, you will be entitled to your $125,000 lifetime exclusion on only a portion of the gain. The portion will be based on the present value of your life estate in proportion to the value of the "remainder interest" (what you have given away) at the time of sale. The owners of the remainder interest (presumably your children) will be taxed on their share of the gain in proportion to the value of their remainder interest.

To Illustrate

> Catherine, age seventy-six, makes a gift of her home to her two children, reserving a life estate for herself. Three years later, Catherine and the children decide to sell the home for $250,000, which represents a total gain of $200,000. According to the IRS tables, Catherine's life estate is worth about 50 percent of the present value of the property. Because Catherine "owns" only 50 percent of the home, she will be able to apply her lifetime exclusion only to that portion of the gain (50 percent × $200,000, or $100,000). Since this gain is under $125,000, Catherine will pay no taxes on it. However, the remainder of the gain ($200,000 less $100,000, or $100,000) will be taxed to the children, and unless they have losses to offset the gain, they'll pay a tax of about $28,000.

Tip

> If you think you may sell the home, don't use the life estate.

Gift taxes: In transferring the home with a reserved life estate, you will have made an irrevocable gift equal to the present value of the remainder interest. The values are usually taken from special IRS or government tables that tell us what percentage of the present value of the gift applies to a remainder interest after the death of a person of a given present age.

To Illustrate

The tables may say that the value of a gift of a remainder interest by a seventy-year-old is presently worth 39 percent of the gift, meaning that if a seventy-year-old gave his son a remainder interest in a $100,000 home, he would be making a *present* gift to the son of $39,000, even though the son won't own the home free and clear until his father's death.

Tip

As noted throughout, the gift tax implications of making gifts in Medicaid planning cases normally is *not* an issue, since a person can give away up to $600,000 without incurring a gift tax.

Estate taxes: Just as gifts with a reserved life estate provide no income tax benefits, the retention of benefits from the gifted property will generally negate any estate tax advantages. For purposes of estate taxes, a gift of this type will cause the full value of the gifted property to be included in the donor's estate for *both* federal and state tax purposes. Given the average size of Medicaid planning cases, however, normally this is not an issue, for in most instances there will be no federal estate tax and only a nominal state estate tax (in those few states that have an estate tax).

Important Note

In many if not most instances, particularly where the home is involved, there is actually an *advantage* to including the property in the estate. It is that the beneficiaries (in this case, the remaindermen) receive the property with a new (stepped-up) cost basis equal to the value of the property for estate tax purposes (usually this is the fair market value at the date of the life tenant's death) whether or not an estate tax is due. In most cases, the effect of this is to eliminate or at least materially reduce the capital gains tax on a later sale of the property by the beneficiaries.

To Illustrate _____

Jack transfers his home to his daughter, Jean, reserving a life estate for himself. The cost of the home, including improvements over the years, totals $50,000. A few years after the transfer, Jack dies, and at his death the home is valued at $265,000. Later, Jean sells the home, realizing about $275,000 in sales proceeds after expenses. Because the home was included in Jack's estate at a value of $265,000 for estate tax purposes, that amount ($265,000) will be Jean's cost basis for the home. Therefore, Jean will have only a capital gain of $10,000 on the sale ($275,000 received less $265,000 cost basis). If the home was *not* included in Jack's estate, then Jean would have to take Jack's original cost basis ($50,000) and the same sale would have resulted in a capital gain of $225,000 to Jean!

Trusts

If a *revocable* trust is used, the federal and state consequences are the same as if you had continued to own the property in your own name. That is, the income taxes are *exactly* the same, no gift has been made, and on your death, the *full* value of the trust is considered part of your estate for estate tax purposes.

Irrevocable trusts for Medicaid purposes are only slightly different:

Income taxes: Since you have reserved the right to income and the right to direct who will receive the remaining assets in the trust on your death, the tax laws provide that all of the income (or losses) of the trust are taxed to you, *whether they are distributed or not.* If you release or relinquish all your rights under the trust, the income may then be taxed to the trust or to some other beneficiary, and you will have made a gift. If a typical irrevocable Medicaid trust (described previously) holds your home and the home is sold, you will be entitled to the *full* $125,000 exclusion from capital gains tax, assuming you and/or your spouse are the only income beneficiaries. (This result is different from that of a sale under a reserved life estate.)

Note

Not all irrevocable Medicaid trusts will preserve the $125,000 capital gains exclusion on the sale of a home. If this is a concern, be sure your lawyer understands the relevant tax issues involved in drafting the trust and the special provisions which must be included to make it a "fully grantor" trust.

Note

If you or your spouse is the trustee of the trust (or if either of you is co-trustee with someone else), then you *DO NOT* need to file a separate income tax return for the trust (whether it is revocable or irrevocable) and you *DO NOT* need a separate trust ID number. If your advisor or your bank tries to tell you otherwise, tell them to look at treasury (IRS) regulations under section 301.6109(a)! However, if *neither* of you is a trustee, then the trust should apply for a separate federal ID number and should file a tax return (called an information return) each year. The information return merely advises the IRS (and, in some cases, the state) that all of the income received by the trust is taxed to you (the grantor of the trust). The trust generally does not pay a separate income tax while either you (the grantor) or your spouse is a beneficiary.

Gift taxes: When you create an irrevocable trust, you are normally making a gift of the remainder interest (what is left after your death), and in most cases there are the usual gift tax considerations involved, as discussed under gifts with a reserved life estate. However, in the case of an irrevocable trust, there is a way to eliminate any gift tax consideration (in case your gifts will exceed the $600,000 allowable amount). Federal gift tax regulations provide that if you retain the right to determine who will receive your property at some later date, you have not made a completed gift of the property at the time of the transfer to the trust. Therefore, if you have your attorney include a provision in the trust giving you a "special testamentary power of appointment," the gift tax issues will be eliminated. In fact, most irrevocable Medicaid trusts contain such a provision.

The special testamentary power of appointment means that you reserve the right to name in your will (testamentary) from among a specified group (say children or grandchildren) those who will receive the balance of your trust on your death. The fact that you *never exercise* the power is unimportant; the mere existence of the power is all that is necessary. In fact, normally, you would *not* exercise the power, but would allow the provisions of the trust to carry out the disposition of the property at your death. The presence of the special power is only to eliminate the gift tax issue.

Important Note

> Having this power to direct the trust assets at your death will not affect your Medicaid eligibility under present law, since you have no right to recover the assets or to pay them to your creditors or your estate.

Estate taxes: As with the income, the retention of benefits from the irrevocable trust during your lifetime will cause the *full value* of the trust property to be included in your estate for federal and state estate tax purposes. But *remember,* the purpose of creating this whole arrangement was *not* to save taxes; it was to preserve and protect the family assets in the event of a catastrophic illness.

Family Limited Partnerships

Once it became clear that the benefit and asset protection offered by irrevocable Medicaid trusts would be gradually taken away, practitioners began to look for and consider other planning tools that might offer similar or even additional benefits, and the Family Limited Partnership began to surface. Though it has not yet become what you might call a household word, the Family Limited Partnership is being considered by some practitioners as an alternative to the Medicaid trust — but with the cautions discussed later.

A partnership is a legal entity formed by two or more individuals who join together to engage in a "business activity" for a profit. A limited partnership is a partnership with one or more general partners and one or more limited partners. A Family Limited Partnership (FLIP) is simply one where all the partners are members of the same family. The general partners are responsible for managing the partnership and are personally liable for all the debts and activities of the partnership, while the limited partners have no say in the management and have only limited liability. Their liability is usually limited to their investment in the partnership. Further, it is usually the general partner who decides *how much* (if any), and *when* partnership income is distributed to the partners. Generally, when income is distributed, the partners (both general and limited) will receive distributions of income in proportion to their shares in the partnership. Finally, the partnership agreement is often drafted so that the limited partners may not transfer or liquidate their shares nor make or order any withdrawals.

Therefore, with a FLIP, the limited partners will only receive distributions that the general partner decides to make and the limited partners cannot force a general partner to make any distributions. Further, the limited partner cannot cash in or withdraw his share or any part of it until the partnership liquidates, which is typically forty to fifty years after its formation.

Important Note _____

Remember that a partnership must have a "business purpose" in order to be valid. While it has been established that investments such as stocks and bonds, income-producing real estate, and perhaps even savings accounts, for a short term, can have a business purpose, your home and your unrented vacation home do *not* have a business purpose and could "taint" an otherwise valid partnership.

Accordingly, an individual who transfers all of her *investment* assets to a FLIP where she has no subsequent control over the assets could argue that such assets have become inaccessible assets and, therefore, should not be counted as a Medicaid resource. She could also argue that the transfer of these assets in exchange for a partnership interest was a transfer for valid consideration, and so she should be eligible for Medicaid immediately.

To my knowledge, this idea has not been tested, at least not on a meaningful scale; therefore, you must review it very carefully with expert counsel before any steps are taken. Furthermore, many of us who have deliberated over the idea are concerned with the provision in the 1993 OBRA change that says "the term *trust* includes any legal instrument or device that is similar to a trust. . . ."

Since an argument could be made that the FLIP is similar to a discretionary trust in that the general partner is a "fiduciary" (like a trustee) who holds the partnership assets for the benefit of the partners (like the beneficiaries), and has the authority to make distributions as he deems appropriate (like a discretionary trust), we may have a "device that is similar to a trust." Therefore, the partnership could simply be treated as a trust by the state and the share attributable to the limited partner/Medicaid applicant will be fully countable as a resource. As they say, "the jury is still out" on this approach.

Important Note

The issue of countability of a person's partnership share may be totally different if the partnership was formed long before the Medicaid issue arose and for reasons that had nothing to do with Medicaid. Many families form FLIPs for estate planning and asset protection reasons and these FLIPs may, in fact, offer Medicaid protection as well. My concerns would lie where an individual used a FLIP as a direct alternative to an irrevocable Medicaid trust, as I believe that would be subject to attack by the state for the reasons explained above.

Unfortunately, in many cases, it will be difficult to tell between the two. For instance, if a person forms a FLIP to which she transfers all her assets (along with assets of other family members), then three years later applies for Medicaid, it will be a question of fact whether the motive for the FLIP was estate planning or Medicaid planning and the burden of proof will be on the applicant.

Divorce or Separation As a Medicaid Planning Tool

Occasionally, catastrophic family circumstances require drastic measures to deal with them. In such cases, the sheer need for survival can drive people to actions they would never have dreamed of taking under normal conditions. Divorce and separation in the face of a catastrophic illness falls into this category.

There can be cases where the only apparent solution for the healthy spouse is to take legal action against the institutionalized spouse for divorce or separate support. This is because a *court order* for the payment of income or the transfer of assets from the institutionalized spouse to the healthy spouse constitutes an *exception* to the otherwise prescribed standards for monthly income allowance or spousal resource allowance under the Medicaid laws.

To Illustrate

Say that John and Mary have assets of $70,000 and a home. However, as a result of John's recent retirement from a partnership, he is slated to receive $4,000 per month in income over a three-year period. Thereafter, he will get a pension of $900 per month. John is institutionalized, and Mary is allowed one-half the assets, or $35,000, as a spousal resource allowance. Mary spends John's $35,000 in about a year, then applies for Medicaid. (Although John's continued income is far in excess of the Medicaid eligibility limit, if he applies the "excess" income toward his nursing home costs, he may still qualify for Medicaid benefits *provided* he does not reside in an income cap state — see discussion of this in Chapter 1.) Mary, who has no other income, is allowed a monthly income allowance of $1,200, which she may take from John's income. The balance of $2,800 per month goes to the nursing home. Two years later, when John's income drops to $900 per month, it won't matter that Mary was allowed $1,200 per month, since the money simply isn't there, and the state certainly won't make up the difference. In the meantime, Mary has spent $35,000 of their assets plus about $70,000 of John's income to pay for his nursing home costs. It doesn't have to be that way.

If, instead, at the time of John's institutionalization, Mary and John agreed to a separation or a divorce, Mary might have obtained a court order directing John to give her a "settlement" of something more than half of the $70,000 in assets. In addition, the court could have ordered John to pay Mary a larger amount, say $3,000 per month, for the three-year period. Such an order would take priority over the spousal resource allowance and the income allowance. In that case, John would have qualified for Medicaid much sooner and Mary would have a lot more security.

The problem with this strategy is that it is far easier to write about it and talk about it than it is to do it. A spouse of twenty-five or forty-five years will undoubtedly find it extremely difficult to publicly sue for separation or divorce. The healthy spouse normally feels that she is "deserting" the ill spouse, even though, we argue, it is only "on paper." And it is bad enough to think about such action when a spouse, even though institutionalized, is competent. If the spouse is incompetent, the situation becomes far more difficult for two reasons.

The first is the emotional trauma of legally abandoning a spouse at a time when because of his incompetence, not to mention his institutionalization, he appears to need the most help. The second is the increased legal complexities of divorcing (or suing for support from) an incompetent spouse. Since the incompetent spouse cannot appear in court for himself, a guardian must be appointed to represent the incompetent spouse. It is then the guardian's legal duty to act only in the best interest of his "ward" (the incompetent spouse), so he may actually be required to oppose the divorce or separation, or at least to *oppose* giving away too much of the ward's property or income, especially since the ward now needs it himself for nursing home costs. Although it is not unheard of to have a court award a favorable settlement to the healthy spouse in such cases, divorce or separate support proceedings against an incompetent spouse are sure to be expensive and are usually employed *only* as a last resort.

Use of the Prenuptial Agreement to Create Individual Assets: The Second-Marriage Dilemma

As discussed in Chapter 2, all the assets of *both* spouses are pooled to determine the amount that may be kept by the healthy spouse and the amount that must be "spent down" by the institutionalized spouse before he can qualify for Medicaid. Contrast this with the old Medicaid rules (that is, before September 30, 1989), under which each spouse could have his or her own individual assets, and after a very brief period, the assets of the healthy spouse would not be counted for Medicaid purposes.

The current pooling of spousal assets rule can have a particularly disastrous effect on spouses of second marriages, especially where the healthy spouse brought substantial assets into the marriage, regards them as her own individual assets, and wants to preserve these assets for her own security. Unfortunately, the pooling of assets rule disregards such considerations and treats all spousal assets as available to *both* spouses. The advent of this rule has generated the question of how to segregate such assets, and, in particular, whether a legally binding prenuptial (or even postnuptial) agreement between the spouses can operate to segregate their assets so that the healthy spouse's assets will not be considered available to the institutionalized spouse. If only it were that simple.

Although prenuptial and postnuptial agreements can be legally binding between the spouses and perhaps even with respect to most third parties, *such agreements are completely ignored when it comes to the pooling of assets rule for Medicaid eligibility purposes.*

Despite the origin of the funds and despite any agreement between spouses, *all* of the assets available to *either* spouse are counted if one spouse becomes institutionalized. If this were not the case, spouses could merely enter into a marital agreement to defeat the Medicaid laws, while still maintaining the freedom of ownership of their assets.

This rule can appear extremely harsh where, for instance, a spouse with children and substantial assets from a first marriage marries a spouse with little or no assets who subsequently becomes institutionalized. A prenuptial agreement offers *no* protection in such cases.

To Illustrate

Before Sam, age sixty-nine, and Sarah, age sixty-two, were married, they had lengthy discussions about their respective responsibilities to their children from their first marriages. Sam had one child and Sarah had three children. They had their attorneys draw up a prenuptial agreement acknowledging that neither would make any claim upon the property of the other, either during their lifetimes or at death. Sarah had about $220,000 in investments and savings (from her first husband's life insurance policies), and Sam had about $32,000 left after the divorce of his first wife. The prenuptial agreements were signed, sealed, and delivered, and Sarah and Sam felt comfortable that their respective assets were protected.

About a year later, however, Sam had a stroke, and it eventually became necessary to place him in a nursing home at a cost of $5,000 per month. When Sarah asked about getting assistance from Medicaid, she was told that she would first have to spend about $175,000 of *her* money before Sam could qualify for Medicaid. Sarah argued that she had a legally binding prenuptial agreement in which Sam agreed not to touch any of her funds. The state informed Sarah that while the agreement might be binding on Sam, it was not binding on the state, and that they would not pay for Sam's nursing home costs until both he *and* Sarah were down to the required amount of assets.

Tip

One solution in such cases is to resort to a legal separation or divorce. Although this is admittedly a drastic move, it is the most reliable way to preserve Sarah's investments. Otherwise she would have to resort to attempts to convert her countable assets into noncountable assets or income. For instance, after

Sarah's spousal resource allowance is established by the state, she could use the balance of the countable funds to purchase an annuity for her lifetime. This would have the effect of converting countable assets to noncountable income for Sarah, and Sam would immediately qualify for Medicaid. (See Case Study 8 in Chapter 11 for more on this idea.)

Note

If a spouse does choose to seek a separation or divorce, it should be done, if at all possible, while the ill spouse is still mentally competent. Obtaining a separation or divorce from an incompetent spouse can be complicated and expensive as explained above.

Personal Injury Settlements

Occasionally a person on Medicaid or expected to be in need of long term care will become entitled to recover damages for personal injuries. This could happen as a result of an injury in a hospital or a nursing home or an accident that caused the need for long term care or an unrelated accident. Each of these may have different implications in terms of Medicaid planning and, therefore, each may require different strategies. In all cases, however, the recovery will normally be a countable asset and, if nothing is done, it will immediately disqualify the individual from receiving benefits. Further, with no plan, the entire recovery is likely to be spent on the individual's care. What follows is a very brief review of the issues and possible solutions, as they relate to Medicaid planning. If you have a case where a suit for personal injuries is planned, already instituted, or about to be settled, it is *imperative* that you seek expert counsel.

If the recovery is for an injury that gave use to the need for long term care, it is almost certain that the Medicaid agency will have a lien (legal claim) on the proceeds up to the amount previously paid to the individual for Medicaid benefits. This is because most states either by law or by their Medicaid applications typically include a "subrogation" right to such recoveries. Subrogation means that as a condition of application for benefits you are allowing the state the right to participate in the claim for recovery. In such cases, there is not much you can do about avoiding reimbursement of the state. Any excess, however, may be the subject of a Medicaid plan, and from that point the approach would be no different than that if other assets were held. That is, outright gifts, an income-only trust, or the purchase of an annuity, as applicable, might be considered. Further, in some situations a carefully planned "structured settlement" can preserve a considerable part of the recovery. (See illustration below.)

Where there is no lien, however, there may be more opportunity for a creative plan. For instance, in some cases, the entire recovery need not go to the disabled individual. It is very common for the spouse of the individual to be entitled to a share of the recovery for "loss of consortium" (companionship). Further, many states allow children or parents of the injured party to make such a claim as well. In these cases, the share that is paid to the spouse, children, or parents does not belong to the individual and never did belong to him, so none of it would be counted as a resource, nor would that share be treated as a disqualifying transfer. The parent, spouse, or children could do with those funds as they pleased, including the establishment of a discretionary trust for the disabled individual's benefit. Note that such trusts can have very complicated tax implications and must be designed and drafted by expert counsel.

As to funds that are paid to or available to the disabled individual, generally these funds will be counted as a resource. Even though the individual may be incompetent and the funds are transferred, for instance, to a trust for the individual's benefit by a guardian under a court order, they will nevertheless be considered as having been transferred *by* the individual and an accompanying disqualification period (likely to be sixty months) will apply.

Despite these exposures, there may be ways to structure the settlement in a fashion that best suits the overall family needs considering the preservation of maximum benefits for the individual.

Caroline, age fifty-five, and divorced, suffered severe personal injuries in an auto accident. She has a daughter, Cindy, age twenty, who cannot care for herself. Caroline's injuries are such that although technically she has a normal life expectancy (about twenty-two years), her doctors predict that complications could easily arise which would bring about her death much earlier. Monthly expenses for her care exceed $8,000 and are paid by Medicaid. There is a Medicaid lien of $200,000 on the potential recovery. Caroline's attorney is negotiating for the recovery.

After extensive negotiations, it is agreed that Caroline will receive a lump sum payment of $225,000 plus additional expenses to recover legal fees, etc., and the balance of the recovery will be paid $2,100 per month for the first five years, then $5,000 per month for the rest of her life, with a term certain of twenty years. If Cynthia dies within the term certain, the payments will be paid to a discretionary trust for the benefit of her disabled daughter.

The effect of this settlement will be to allow Caroline to remain on Medicaid, while paying only the lien and fraction of the cost of her continued care. If she dies before the twenty-year term, payments will continue to be made to her daughter's benefit without claim by Medicaid.

If Caroline had taken a lump sum instead of a structured settlement, under the best of conditions she would have to pay the $8,000 per month for at least sixty months (if she established a trust — the likely outcome) or thirty-six months if she gave away most of the settlement (a highly unlikely outcome), for costs, respectively, of $480,000 (for sixty months) and $228,000 (for thirty-six months). It is far more likely that a court would approve the structured settlement as it provides for Caroline for her lifetime and does not require any irrevocable gifts of her funds.

There can be many different scenarios and planning arrangements to suit them, where personal injury settlements are involved. The key is to investigate the possibilities through expert counsel BEFORE the settlement takes place.

Reverse Mortgages

I include the reverse mortgage here not because I see it as a Medicaid planning strategy but rather because many others mistakenly do, and they will be looking for it in this book, if not this chapter.

A reverse mortgage is a loan given (usually) by a bank on the equity value of a person's home. It is called a "reverse" mortgage because instead of taking a lump sum loan and then paying the lender back in installments (typically in monthly mortgage payments) over a number of years, it is just the reverse. The lender pays *you* monthly installments over a number of years, and *you* then pay the lump sum when the monthly payments stop. Typically this means a forced sale of the home on which the reverse mortgage was granted, and this is one of the problems.

Another problem is that while the monthly payments can of course help an at-home spouse with little or no income, the effect of that is to reduce the income she might otherwise be granted as her monthly income allowance by Medicaid, and also to expose that income to her costs of care if she should later enter a nursing home. Further, it ties up the home since no intrafamily transfers could be made without paying off the mortgage. In short, while the reverse mortgage may be helpful in non-Medicaid situations, I do not consider it an attractive strategy to be used in Medicaid planning.

To summarize, there are many different accepted and legal strategies to protect assets for Medicaid purposes. While the numerous strategies explained in this chapter are comprehensive, it is impossible to list every nuance of each strategy or to predict future strategies that may be developed as federal regulations and state practices become clearer. Further, it has been my experience that in most cases a combination of strategies is indicated to achieve the "best" plan under the circumstances. Therefore, although it is essential that you understand the options available to you, you should not try to implement your own plan; there is no substitute for expert counsel.

CHAPTER FIVE

Long Term Care Insurance: What to Look for in a Policy

*T*he "simple" solution to the whole problem of Medicaid and nursing home or other "custodial care" costs actually appears to be quite easy. Just go out and purchase an insurance policy that covers your long term care costs!

Unfortunately, that may be the tough part of the easy solution. Though there are a myriad of apparently reputable companies offering proposed answers to all of our long term insurance needs, many experts who have studied the question believe that it is difficult to find a single policy that meets all desirable requirements from an insurance and long term care viewpoint at a reasonable cost, and at least one expert feels that even if there are such policies, the insurance companies will eventually be unable to pay on them because so many policyholders will be in nursing homes.

Most policies, for example, purport to have "fixed" premium rates, but at the same time the policy states that the rates may be increased, so long as there is a corresponding increase in the rates for everyone in the same class. Others exclude Alzheimer's disease, which is one of the most common causes of the need for custodial care. Still others require a period of hospitalization before the policy will pay benefits, though a substantial percentage of nursing home admissions are not preceded by hospitalization. Nevertheless, through a careful screening process and with the help of professional advice you can trust, you should be able to find a policy that at least adequately covers you through the "initial period" if not longer.

By initial period I refer to the thirty-six-month (or possibly sixty-month) waiting period between the transfer of assets and Medicaid eligibility. For people who don't want to give their money away or tie everything up in trusts, a policy paying for the first thirty-six months of nursing home costs would allow them to wait until the time of the institutionalization to transfer their assets (most policies offer a pay period option of thirty-six months). After the thirty-six-month period they would then qualify for Medicaid. Of course, it is important that proper arrangements be made to facilitate a transfer as soon as possible after the policy begins to pay for nursing home costs. In the case of assets in a trust, virtually no change or transfer of assets would need to be made, but a longer waiting period—up to sixty months—may apply. For assets outside a trust, however, it would be *important* that institutionalized persons have executed a durable power of attorney (see my discussion in Chapter 6 on the durable power of attorney).

To Illustrate

> Bill purchased a policy that will pay his nursing home costs for up to thirty-six months after he enters a nursing home. He does no other planning with his assets, except that he does sign a durable power of attorney over to his wife, Barbara. Bill develops a condition that requires nursing home care. Shortly after Bill enters the nursing home, Barbara uses the durable power of attorney to transfer all of Bill's (and her own) assets in excess of about $75,000, to their children. Thirty-six months after the transfer (when the insurance runs out), Bill will be eligible for Medicaid benefits.

Of course, there are other issues to consider here, and perhaps even other strategies. For instance, if Barbara wanted to keep the income from their savings, she could transfer the assets to an income-only trust. However, this could necessitate up to a sixty-month wait and Bill's costs of care during the waiting period would have to be considered. Instead, she could also consider the purchase of an annuity as explained in Chapter 3.

In selecting the long term care policy that suits your needs, you should consider the following issues, which, although not exhaustive, will help you separate the acceptable long term care policy from the unacceptable:

1. What expenses are covered? Does the policy cover only skilled care provided by doctors, nurses, and therapists? Some policies cover even home care. A good policy would cover skilled, intermediate, custodial, *and* home care.

2. Is there a waiting period? Many policies do not begin paying until a waiting period of anywhere from ten days to one hundred days has elapsed. Don't rely on Medicare to pay the first one hundred days, since Medicare will pay only if you are in a *skilled* nursing facility (SNF) *and* in a "bed" in that particular home that qualifies under Medicare regulations. In fact, most nursing facilities are not certified by Medicare, and chances are that you would not be covered under the waiting period. Therefore, look for a shorter waiting period.

3. What is the benefit limitation? Benefits are almost always limited, either in periods of time or in dollar amounts paid. Some policies add a further limitation of a percentage of costs incurred (such as 80 percent of actual nursing home costs). Note also that many policies even offer automatic benefits that are realistic in view of approximate nursing home costs. Obviously, the more generous the benefits, the greater the premiums you'll pay, so be sure to compare "apples to apples." Also keep in mind that *most* nursing home stays are for *less* than thirty-six months (which is one reason the Medicaid law requires a thirty-six-month wait). If you are tying the policy coverage to a possible transfer of assets later on, then you won't need more than thirty-six or sixty months' coverage, but this should *not* be the only deciding factor.

4. Does the policy exclude a preexisting condition? This is not an unreasonable exclusion, since the idea of insurance is to purchase it before you need it. If people could purchase policies after the fact, insurance companies would not exist. Even those policies with exclusions for preexisting conditions, however, often eliminate the exclusion after a period of six months to one year or more.

5. *Does the policy require a prior hospitalization?* A good many policies will pay nursing home or other benefits only if the individual was in a hospital for at least two or three days prior to entering the home. This practice exists because more than half the people entering nursing homes do not require a hospital stay first, making the risk much less for the insurance company. If possible, therefore, select a policy without this requirement or pay a little extra to have it waived.

6. *What is not covered?* Most policies, or at least the corresponding promotional material, will clearly state what is *not* covered by the policy. They usually exclude, among other things, care costs resulting from mental or nervous disorders, unless it can be shown that such costs are the result of an organic disorder. Also often excluded are Alzheimer's disease, Parkinson's disease, and senility. If the policy is not clear on these points, be sure to ask, since these are among the more common causes of long term care needs.

7. *Can the premiums be increased?* Most policies provide that the premiums you pay will not be increased *unless* (and this could prove to be a big "unless" if your particular company happens to have too many of its customers enter nursing homes) the rates for everyone are increased. Otherwise, the premiums you are quoted when signing up will be the same every year and will *not* increase with your age. In addition to the no-increase concern, make sure that future premiums are waived (no longer need to be paid) in the event of permanent disability or institutionalization.

8. *Can the policy be canceled by the insurer?* Most recent policies claim to be "guaranteed renewable" so long as you pay your premiums. (Many have a waiver of premiums provision while you are in a nursing home.) Do not purchase a policy that is renewable at the option of the insurer.

9. *Does the policy have an inflation rider?* Although $150

per day coverage may seem like enough right now, what happens when five years from now the same costs are $210 per day and you cannot change your policy because of the onset of an illness? Many policies have (or have available for a cost) an inflation rider which causes the policy benefit to automatically increase to keep pace with inflation. However, be sure to compare the cost of the inflation rider to the cost of simply increasing the coverage at the outset (to, say, $200 or $225 per day). It could be cheaper to do the latter.

10. Is the insurer reputable? This is an important factor to consider. Large, reputable companies do have an image and reputation to maintain. In case of a dispute, at least you know the company will be there and will try to maintain its reputation in the industry. Try to stay away from those like "Ralph's Vinyl Siding and Long Term Care Insurance Company." *Consumer Reports* magazine suggests that you look for a company with an A. M. Best rating of A or A+ (A. M. Best is a company that grades the financial status of insurance companies).

Unfortunately, even a big name and a high rating are not guarantees of a good policy. Many states have established policy guidelines that a company must meet before it can sell its individual (as opposed to group) long term care policies in the state. These guidelines are designed to protect the consumer and should eventually contribute to true long term care protection under most circumstances, but only time will tell.

Note

State regulations and guidelines generally protect you on *individual* policies but often have little effect on *group* policies, such as those offered to you "at a special price," because you are a member of the United States Citizens Club. Beware of these special deals; have them reviewed by your advisors before you buy.

Finally, you should be aware of a new trend in insurance called "Living Benefits." This is an arrangement whereby the face value of a *life* insurance policy may be withdrawn by the insured and used to pay such things as medical or nursing home costs.

To Illustrate

> Ben has a life insurance policy that will pay $15,000 on Ben's death. Ben is very ill and in a nursing home but is not eligible for Medicaid. If Ben's state insurance commission has approved a Living Benefits program, Ben would be able to withdraw up to the entire $15,000 policy amount to pay for his care.

Generally, to be able to make such a withdrawal, the insured person must be certified to be terminally ill or have a life expectancy of less than two years, or be in need of a major organ transplant. Therefore, use of this benefit is infrequent.

Although a majority of states have adopted the Living Benefits program, it is clearly not the answer to all your long term care needs. In many, if not most, cases, the more traditional long term care policy should be considered.

As stated at the outset, there may be no perfect long term care policy, but you should be able to find a policy that can offer you most if not all of the protection you seek, at least for the initial thirty-six-month period. Together with your attorney and insurance advisor, you should review what the policy offers you and compare its features with the guidelines in this chapter; then, assuming you have decided to purchase long term care insurance, choose the one from the most reputable company that comes closest to your needs.

CHAPTER SIX

Durable Power of Attorney: Don't Leave Home Without It!

A durable power of attorney is perhaps one of the *most* important (and least expensive) documents you can have in your estate plan, *particularly* in the case of Medicaid planning, and it is generally agreed among the best estate attorneys that a durable power of attorney should be a part of every estate plan.

For a cost of generally under $200, a well-drafted durable power of attorney can easily save a family hundreds or even thousands of dollars in legal fees and other costs that it might face when one of its members becomes incompetent. Despite its potential value, however, the durable power is often overlooked or even rejected by people who feel they don't need one because everything they own is held in joint names with a spouse or with another close family member. This belief can lead to trouble.

To Illustrate

Many people are under the mistaken impression that all assets held in joint names with another person can easily be accessed or sold or transferred by either owner. This may be true of joint bank accounts, but that's about it. A joint tenant *cannot* refinance, sell, or transfer jointly owned real estate or jointly registered securities without the consent of the other joint owner.

If a joint owner becomes incompetent, therefore, the other joint owner (or some other party) must petition the probate court to have a guardian or conservator appointed for the property but also for any other property held in the name of the incompetent person alone. However, the expensive and time-consuming probate court proceedings can be avoided if, *before* a person becomes incompetent, he signs a durable power of attorney.

For Medicaid planning purposes, a properly drafted durable power of attorney can often save the family from poverty. Having a durable power of attorney usually enables a family member to carry out or complete the Medicaid planning transfers or other maneuvers that the incompetent person did not do while he or she was competent. *But this will work only if the power is a durable one.*

What Is a Power of Attorney?

A regular power of attorney is a written instrument signed by you through which you legally authorize someone else to act for you if you are not present. Legally, the power-holder becomes your *agent*. The problem with a regular power of attorney is that if you become legally incompetent, the power, for all practical purposes, would automatically *cease* to have legal effect, despite the fact that this is just when you need it most.

To Illustrate

Say that you give your son, Bill, who is caring for you, a regular power of attorney, allowing him, in so many words, to do everything you could do if you were present. Later you become incompetent, and it is necessary and advisable for Bill to deed certain property out of your name. He could *not* legally do this, even though he has your power of attorney, because, with only certain exceptions, the nondurable power of attorney is *automatically terminated* when you become incompetent.

In order to make the transfer after your incompetence, your son (or some other interested party) would be required to petition the probate court, asking that you be declared legally incompetent and that a guardian or conservator be appointed in your behalf. Once the guardian is appointed, the guardian would then have to take further legal action to ask the court's permission to transfer the property, after explaining to the court's satisfaction why such a transfer was necessary. Meanwhile, all interested parties, including your heirs, would receive notice of each of these proceedings, offering them the opportunity to object.

This was the law for hundreds of years (and still is if you fail to plan), until lawmakers finally recognized the need for a power that survived a person's incompetence, and the *durable* power of attorney gradually came into being. Now all states and the District of Columbia recognize some form of durable power of attorney. (Later in this chapter I note some states' special rules on durable powers of attorney.)

A durable power of attorney is simply a regular power of attorney with the added statement or provision that the power you have given will not be terminated or affected by your subsequent disability or incapacity. (Another form of durable power, discussed in the next section, takes effect *at the time of* your disability or incapacity.) The person you name to act for you under the power is called your *"attorney in fact,"* which simply means your agent.

Scope of the Power

A power of attorney can be extremely broad or it can be limited to specific acts or transactions. The power can authorize your attorney in fact to sign checks, enter contracts, buy or sell real estate, deposit or withdraw funds, buy or sell stocks or bonds, enter safe-deposit boxes, file suits on your behalf, create or amend trusts, file tax returns, make disclaimers of inheritances, run your business, make gifts and other transfers of property that you might have made, deal with jointly held property, and do just about anything else that you could have done, all without the need of seeking probate court permission to do so, though you cannot delegate the power to make a will.

For Medicaid planning purposes, the power should not only be very broad, containing the provisions outlined above, but it should also contain specific wishes or instructions to your attorney in fact relating to specific assets, when appropriate. For instance, under the provision allowing for gifts, the document might say, "If my attorney in fact deems it in the best interests of my family, I direct that my interest in my residence situated at 1100 Main Street, Centerville, be transferred to my wife, Helen, outright or in such form as she may choose."

And speaking of gifts, if you wish your attorney in fact to have the power to make gifts (remember, it is essential for Medicaid planning purposes), *it must be specifically included in the document.* The power "to do everything I could do . . ." is *not* sufficient. Furthermore, if your attorney in fact is a spouse or other close relative, be sure the document specifically allows her or him to be a donee of such gifts (*assuming* that is what you wish). In short, go to an attorney who knows what he or she is doing—this is not a place for amateurs and *especially* not for tear-out forms from a do-it-yourself book.

Perhaps one of the more significant advantages of the durable power is that it can allow (or even instruct) your attorney in fact to make gifts or to transfer assets to a trust for your benefit or for your family's benefit. The trust could be a Medicaid type of trust, designed to preserve family assets in the event of long term illness. As the following illustration shows, this may be more advantageous in the long run than simply making outright transfers to a spouse because your trust could also provide for protection of the funds in the event of your spouse's possible illness, whereas an outright transfer of funds to your spouse would expose those funds to Medicaid in the event your spouse later entered a nursing home.

To Illustrate

Say that John becomes incompetent and may soon have to enter a nursing home. He has $300,000 worth of countable assets and had previously executed a durable power of attorney, naming his son, Jack, as attorney in fact and giving Jack the express authority to make gifts or to transfer all of John's funds to an irrevocable trust. The trust could provide that John and his wife, Mary, could receive whatever amounts of *income* were necessary for their comfort and care. However, in the event that John enters a nursing home, the trustee could make only payments of *income* to *Mary.* If Mary subsequently entered a nursing home, payments of income could continue for Mary's benefit or for the benefit of both John and Mary until the principal was distributed to the children, depending on the family's decision when creating the trust (for more details on this, see the discussion on trusts in Chapter 4).

After the appropriate waiting period (up to sixty months) this arrangement would avoid using additional funds for Mary's care, but, at the same time, if she never entered a nursing home, she would continue to have the income from the funds for the rest of her life. The effect of the transfer to the irrevocable trust would be to use no more than the trust income for nursing home care for the spouses and, thereafter, to protect and preserve the balance of the principal for the family.

Important Note

Once Jack transferred the funds to the trustee of John's trust using the durable power of attorney, he would have nothing further to do with them, but he would still have authority to deal with any other assets belonging to John *outside* the trust.

Obviously, giving someone so much authority through a durable power of attorney is a two-edged sword. While it ensures privacy and can save money and avoid publicity, the durable power of attorney places tremendous powers in the hands of your attorney in fact. Actually, he could wipe you out with little trouble, and your only recourse would be to sue him for breach of his duty to act only in your behalf (if you could find him). So be careful whom you select as your attorney in fact. Some advisors feel that a fair safeguard to this potential problem is for you to name *two* attorneys in fact, who must act together in your behalf. This will at least reduce the risk, but it also necessitates two signatures on every transaction in order for this precaution to work.

Tip

> If you do name more than one attorney in fact, be sure that your power of attorney *clearly* spells out whether they must act in concert or whether they may act individually, and, in the former case, what happens if one of them is unable to act. I do *not* recommend naming more than two attorneys in fact. It can get quite messy and expensive if they do not agree with one another.

The Springing Power of Attorney

Another option is to have a durable power of attorney that does not become effective until a doctor certifies in writing that you are unable to care for yourself. This is called a "springing" power and will at least defer the risk of being wiped out until you become incompetent, and by then perhaps it won't matter to you. Personally, I think springing powers only invite legal questions regarding the timing and continuance of the power, as well as the verification of your incompetence. For instance, exactly when did you become incompetent—the date of the doctor's letter? Is one letter enough? And what if you later regain your competence? Is it clear that the power continues, or does a person dealing with your attorney in fact have to verify that you are still incompetent? Although some attorneys feel these concerns can be dealt with through special provisions contained in the document, this simply seems to make it more complicated and subject to question. For all these reasons, I dislike springing powers of attorney and almost never recommend them.

Note

> Some states are beginning to recognize these practical problems and at least one (California) has revised its durable power

of attorney law to allow a party designated in the power to declare in writing that the triggering event has occurred.

Tip

If you do *not* want the power to be granted currently, but also want to avoid the complications of a springing power, I recommend having the instrument confer the power at the time it is signed, but *holding* the instrument (that is, do not hand it over to the attorney in fact) until some later date or when the incompetence comes about. In the meantime, it can be left with your lawyer.

To Illustrate

Say that a person signs a durable power of attorney, naming a spouse or a child as attorney in fact. Without the original instrument or a copy of the signed instrument, the spouse or child has no authority to act. In the meantime, the original can be left with the person's lawyer with instructions to deliver it to the spouse or child upon the lawyer's receipt of a letter from the person's physician stating that the person is unable to handle his own affairs. This would avoid the risk of giving the named attorney in fact the power to act too soon and would also avoid third-party questions as to whether the person was, in fact, incompetent, since the durable power does not require that he be incompetent before it takes effect.

Important Note

Your durable power of attorney should also provide for a *successor* attorney in fact if your first-named attorney in fact ceases to serve. And if appointment of a guardian or conservator becomes necessary, in some states you can also nominate your own guardian or conservator in the instrument. (Prior to the enactment of the durable power laws, you were not able to select your own guardian or conservator.)

Another Important Note

Even though you may name (nominate subject to court approval) your own guardian or conservator in the durable power of attorney, this does not mean that it will be necessary to have one appointed should you become incompetent. It could be that the existence of the durable power of attorney will actually *avoid* the necessity for appointment of a guardian or conservator.

You should also note that if a guardian or conservator is appointed, he or she will have the right to *revoke* the power of attorney, and in some states (for example, Connecticut and South Carolina) the appointment of a guardian or conservator *automatically* revokes the power of attorney.

Regardless of its flexibility and advantages, however, you should remember that a durable power of attorney *ceases to have effect at your death*. It is *not* a substitute for a living trust, and although it will help avoid probate during your lifetime (in the event of your incompetence), it will *not* cause assets to avoid probate on your death, as a trust can.

Revoking the Power of Attorney and Dealing with Third Parties

Although it is quite easy to cancel or revoke a power of attorney from a legal standpoint, doing so can present some real problems from a practical standpoint. Legally, all you have to do is notify the attorney in fact that you have canceled the power and ask him to return the original to you. But what if he has kept a copy? Third parties such as banks and stockbrokers generally accept photocopies of the power. And how could you possibly notify every bank and stockholder in the world? (Not to mention other parties who may deal with the attorney in fact.) Even in those few states that require that the durable power of attorney be recorded, similar practical problems can arise.

In short, I know of no real safeguard to this problem other than to spread the risk a little by naming more than one attorney in fact, and in any event to be extremely careful and selective in choosing your attorneys in fact. Another step is to notify all those parties with whom you know you have accounts, such as banks, brokers, and other financial institutions.

As a general rule, most banks, brokers, and certain other parties (such as purchasers of real estate) will require an affidavit from the attorney in fact certifying that you have not revoked the power and that you are still alive. (Some show their ignorance by requiring a statement that you are still competent!) In order to help deal with third parties in this context, most well-drafted powers contain a provision that protects third parties who deal in good faith with the attorney in fact. One problem we occasionally see with using durable powers is the refusal of some third parties to honor them, usually out of ignorance or just an unreasonable policy. If you encounter this problem (often it happens with a bank or a transfer agent) it helps to be insistent and ask to speak to someone from the legal department. In most cases, the firm's attorney will either recognize the validity of the power and OK the transaction, or she will help solve the "policy" problem by telling you what must be done. A few states (but a very few, including New York, Alaska, Minnesota, and California) actually have laws imposing liability on third parties who refuse to honor valid durable powers of attorney.

Signing Several Powers of Attorney

Instead of naming two or more attorneys in fact on one power, some individuals feel comfortable signing two or more durable powers naming a different attorney in fact on each one. Legally, this is permissible, but, practically, be careful. If the attorneys in fact don't agree (and you are incompetent), it could be a race to the bank or broker to see who can get control of your money first, and then a long-term battle to see who is right.

Out-of-State Powers of Attorney

Most states will honor a durable power that was validly executed in the state of your domicile, and at least one state, California, specifically recognizes such a power under its law. This may work for bank accounts or tangible property in the "foreign" state, but it may not be any help where real estate is concerned. State laws regarding transfers of real estate are very precise and a durable power that is valid in one state may not be sufficient to transfer real estate located in another state. Therefore, if you have real estate in more than one state, it would be a good idea to execute separate durable powers of attorney, each complying with the law of the foreign state with respect to durable powers *and* the laws regarding transfers of real estate.

Compensating the Attorney in Fact

Usually the attorney in fact is a spouse or other close relative and so compensation is not an issue. Nevertheless, as a "fiduciary," the attorney in fact is entitled to reasonable compensation for the services rendered. What is reasonable depends upon the circumstances and the nature of the services rendered, but factors to be considered include the time involved, the responsibility, and the urgency of the matter. It is acceptable, though not necessary, to include a provision such as "My attorney in fact shall be entitled to reasonable compensation for the services rendered in my behalf."

Some States' Special Rules for Durable Power of Attorney

Not surprisingly, the laws relating to durable powers of attorney can vary from state to state—for instance, Arkansas, Missouri, North and South Carolina, and Wyoming are states that require some form of *recording* of the durable power for it to be effective. Rhode Island, South Carolina, and Connecticut require witnesses to the durable power. In Minnesota, a spouse acting under a durable power may not sign a deed or certain other real estate documents for the other spouse. In Connecticut, appointment of a guardian automatically *revokes* the durable power; in most other states such a fiduciary merely has the power to revoke. Not all states require that durable power be notarized, but it is standard practice and always advisable. Since the individual states' laws vary so much on the execution of a durable power of attorney, it is a good idea *not* to use one out of a form book, but rather to go to an attorney who specializes in this type of planning. Do *not* risk your estate on a preprinted form to save yourself a few dollars!

Durable Power of Attorney for Health Care

Although powers of attorney are normally used to manage a person's property, a trend has developed toward using the durable power of attorney to appoint an individual to make health care decisions for the person granting the power. In a number of states the power to appoint a person to make health care decisions is allowed by statute. However, even in these states that do not have a specific statute allowing a health care power of attorney, it is generally believed that the courts would honor a person's clearly stated wishes to this effect, unless prohibited by state law.

The health care durable power should be a *separate* document from your regular durable power of attorney. Each performs a very different function and can involve different people (a person to make decisions about your health care and one for your property), so I do *not* recommend trying to combine them.

The power to make health care decisions normally includes the power to decide whether you should undergo any form of medical or other treatment or procedure intended to treat or diagnose any illness or improve any function of the body, whether physical or mental. However, it could also extend the power to decide whether to continue or withhold life-sustaining measures. In my opinion, this second power is more appropriately placed in a *living will*. (A living will is a written declaration of your wishes with respect to the application or continuation of artificial life-support systems in the event that you are diagnosed as terminally ill and that death is considered imminent. Not all states recognize living wills, but those that do also require that the document be signed by the person making it and witnessed by two disinterested persons.)

If you decide to execute a durable power of attorney for health care, it should be signed before two disinterested witnesses unrelated to you and, if possible, notarized. In most states, a non–health care durable power of attorney need only be signed and notarized.

Like any other delegation of authority, a health care power can be revoked, and you can also name a person to succeed the first person if he or she cannot perform the function. As in a regular durable power of attorney, the health care power may take effect immediately or it may become effective at such time as you are unable to make such decisions for yourself. If the latter, the document should be very clear about the time this is deemed to occur (normally on the written certification by at least one physician that such is the case).

Tip

> As with any document of such importance, do not attempt to prepare a durable power of attorney yourself without the help of an advisor experienced in the field. Too much is at stake.

CHAPTER SEVEN

Planning for an Incompetent Person

$\mathcal{T}$he ideal time to plan, of course, is *before* the problems of illness and long term care arise. Often, however, even after an illness comes about, there is still time to plan, since the ill person is still mentally competent to act or direct others to act for him. Unfortunately, once the person becomes incompetent, the number of planning options drops dramatically.

In the eyes of the law, a person is presumed to be competent until he is adjudicated incompetent by the probate court. This does not mean, however, that you simply need to get the questionably competent person to sign his name and the transaction will be "legal." Lawyers, notaries, and anyone else dealing with a person have a certain degree of responsibility to be reasonably aware of the condition and competence of the person they are dealing with. You would not, for example, enter into a contract with an eighty-year-old who has advanced Alzheimer's disease to deed his home to you for $50. The deed would be void since the person did not understand the nature and consequences of his acts, even though he had never been formally declared incompetent by a probate court.

As noted earlier, if a person has signed a properly drafted durable power of attorney and later becomes incompetent, it will be possible for the attorney in fact named under the power to carry out certain transfers or Medicaid planning maneuvers on behalf of the incompetent person and his family.

However, even in cases of incompetence where no durable power of attorney was executed, there may still be opportunities to preserve the family assets, and these should not be overlooked. In this context, the following are some observations and planning techniques that may be considered in cases where the individual is already incompetent and there is no usable durable power of attorney.

Guardianship and Conservatorship

When the individual can no longer understand the nature and consequences of his acts and has not previously signed a durable power of attorney, the only recourse is to ask the court to appoint a guardian or conservator to become the legal representative of the incompetent person.

Generally, where Medicaid and long term care issues are involved, a guardian is more advisable than a conservator, who is charged only with the management of the person's property, while a guardian is given authority over the individual's person and property. (Because it is usually a guardian rather than a conservator who is appointed in long term care cases, from here on I will simply refer to the appointed fiduciary as "the guardian," although the discussion and substantive rules generally apply *equally* to guardian and conservator.)

Appointment of a guardian requires proof to the court that the person is not able to care for himself or able to look after his own affairs. This is usually accomplished by submitting to the court the treating physician's certification that this is the case and any other pertinent evidence. All "interested parties" (that is, all heirs of the person, such as the spouse and children) and, in many states, the state Department of Mental Health, should receive notice of the hearing. In addition, the court will normally appoint someone to represent the individual himself to help ensure that there is no "funny business" involved in asking for the appointment.

The individual appointed by the court is usually called a "guardian ad litem" (GAL), and his job is solely to protect the interests of the allegedly incompetent person. Once the GAL is satisfied that the appointment of a guardian is in fact in the best interests of the individual, he will make a favorable report to the court, and, assuming there are no other objections, the court will then allow the petition and appoint the guardian. At that point, the GAL's assignment is completed, and he will be discharged by the court until further needed. Normally, his fees are paid from the estate of the individual (now called the "ward").

Once the guardian is appointed, he must then give an account to the court of all the assets owned by the ward, as well as any assets in which the ward has an interest. The guardian is then responsible for managing those assets for the ward's benefit. Thereafter, the guardian must file a successive account each year (or more often if the court requires it), showing what came in, what went out (and why), and what is left. If the accounts are to be allowed by the court, a GAL is appointed to review them for the court. As always, interested parties are given the opportunity to object to the guardian's account for valid reasons (such as mismanagement of funds or excessive fees, for example). If the ward's assets are not extensive, it is not unusual in some states for the guardian to file several years' accounts at once instead of filing one every year.

The guardian's powers in dealing with the person's property are carefully restricted by law. Generally, the guardian cannot make distributions of the ward's principal or any major investment changes without the court's express permission and after notice has been given to interested parties. In short, *guardianship can make Medicaid planning very difficult.* These are some of the reasons why most estate attorneys recommend the guardianship to be sought only as a last resort.

Planning Options under Guardianship

Although planning flexibility is extremely limited after a guardian has been appointed, in some cases there are still possibilities. A few state courts recognize the ward's legal obligations of support to other members of his family, and this should not be overlooked as a potential planning tool. For example, Massachusetts has a special statute that *requires* the guardian to provide not only for the ward but also for the "comfortable and suitable maintenance and support" of the ward's *family*. Colorado has a similar but even more permissive law allowing the probate court to create revocable or irrevocable trusts to provide for the care of the incompetent person and the protection of his assets. Other states that have specific statutes allowing gifts or the establishment of some form of planning for the ward include Arkansas, New Jersey, Iowa, Wyoming, Nevada, North Carolina, Connecticut, New York, Texas, Oklahoma, Illinois, and Virginia.

In Medicaid situations it is seldom that minor or other dependent children are involved, but not impossible. If this is the case, a court order should immediately be requested, either under the authority of the applicable statute or under the general authority of the state's probate court, asking that a certain amount of the ward's funds be set aside for the care and support of such dependents. If there are no dependent children but only a spouse, it is also permissible to pay for her support from the ward's funds, assuming it is reasonable and appropriate under the circumstances (that is, that she needs it).

Perhaps the most significant Medicaid planning option, in states that have specific laws that allow it, is the opportunity for a guardian to petition the court to carry out an *estate plan* for the ward. Even in those states that do not have a specific statute allowing the guardian to plan for the ward (see list of states above), every state gives its probate court authority to consider *any* petition filed by a guardian that is in the best interests of the ward and his family. Such a petition might include a request to create trusts, change beneficiaries of insurance policies, purchase annuities, or make other arrangements that are consistent with the intentions of the ward and the needs of the ward and his family.

To Illustrate

Say that John, a widower, age seventy-three, developed advanced Alzheimer's disease and entered a nursing home three years ago. His only assets are his home, worth $200,000 (no mortgage), and a negligible amount of savings. He has a son, Bill, and a daughter, June. June has lived with John for the past ten years and took care of him up to the time he entered the nursing home. John has been on Medicaid since he entered the nursing home. John's home is an exempt asset and, therefore, its value is not counted for Medicaid purposes. John has been incompetent for some time, and John's son was appointed as his guardian. Under the Medicaid law, when John dies the state can place a lien on the assets in John's probate estate and can recover all Medicaid benefits paid to John.

Since the home is in John's name alone (it was jointly owned with his wife, but she is deceased), it will now be a part of his probate estate. The estate, therefore, will be able to force a sale of the home on John's death to recover the Medicaid benefits paid to John.

Because June lived with John for more than two years before he entered the nursing home and since it can be shown that June's care kept John from being institutionalized sooner, a transfer to June falls under one of the exceptions allowed for the transfer of the home. Therefore, John could transfer his home to June without penalty, and the home could be saved. However, Bill, as guardian, does not have the authority to do this without court permission. The plan could be accomplished by filing a petition with the probate court requesting authority to carry out the transfer. If allowed (and there is no reason it should not be allowed), John will remain on Medicaid and the home will belong to June without penalty and free of the Medicaid lien.

Note

In such cases, the local Medicaid agency would be an "interested party" and would be required to receive notice of the petition and a chance to be heard. It would be no surprise if they objected to the plan, but it has been our experience that such objections can be overcome, since the very existence of the exception to the transfer rule can be viewed as a suggestion that this type of transfer is appropriate.

In the above scenario, the only asset, or at least the principal asset, was the home, which, despite its substantial value, is treated differently from other assets. This is not only because of its importance in providing shelter for the spouse and family but because there is the possibility, however remote, that the ward could recover from his illness or be able to even temporarily live there. If instead of a $220,000 home there were $220,000 of investments, the situation would be quite different. That is, it is usually difficult to convince a judge that taking funds *away* from the ward is in the ward's best interests. In such cases, however, there is still the possibility of filing a petition with the probate court to do some Medicaid planning.

To Illustrate

Say that Peter has $350,000 in savings and investments and is about to enter a nursing home at a net cost (after applying Peter's income) of $30,000 per year. His wife, Paula, has been appointed guardian and continues to live in their rented apartment. Her assets are not substantial. Paula could consider the following:

1. Asking the court to allow her to create an irrevocable trust for the benefit of herself, under which she would receive only the income for her life. She would set aside approximately $130,000 to be held outside the trust to pay for Peter's care for the next sixty months (actually, it might be less than sixty months depending upon the cost of care in their state—see discussion on this in Chapter 3). The balance of $220,000 would be transferred to the trust. This arrangement would provide enough to pay for Peter's nursing home cost for the "qualifying" (sixty-month) period, and thereafter he (through his guardian) could apply for Medicaid. If Paula should die, the trust income could revert to Peter for his life. On Peter's death, the assets would pass to the children.

2. Asking the court to allow Paula to *purchase a home* for the family. The cost of the home should be an amount which would leave adequate funds to cover the maintenance, taxes, and so forth of the home, and also leave something

for Peter's care. For instance, if she purchased a home for $200,000, this would leave $150,000 to generate additional income for the other costs. Granted, that amount would not generate enough income for everything, but would likely cover the costs of maintaining the home plus an additional sum for living expenses. Because the home would be an exempt asset, the only assets that would be counted for purposes of Medicaid eligibility would be the remaining $150,000, *less* Paula's $75,000 spousal resource allowance. However, as discussed earlier, Paula can justify an *increase* in her allowance, probably up to the full $150,000, because it would take at least that amount to generate enough income to provide for her monthly income needs (including maintenance of the home). If the state refused to increase her allowance, she could ask the court to allow her to purchase an annuity with the balance. It is quite likely, therefore, that if this plan were allowed by the court and carried out, Peter would almost immediately qualify for Medicaid benefits, while Paula would have a home plus some income.

3. As a last resort, Paula could seek a divorce or, preferably, a separate support order, whereby the court would "order" Peter to transfer assets to Paula or to provide a specified amount of income to her, or both. As discussed earlier, court orders for support or property settlements are exceptions to the spousal income and resource allowances provided under Medicaid laws, so that Paula could have additional funds and Peter could eventually qualify for benefits.

This is not an exhaustive list of every conceivable option available under the above circumstances. Family situations usually differ, as do the opinions and reactions of different judges and the laws (and attitudes) in the various states. And, regardless of the number of options that may appear to be available under a guardianship, it must be remembered that each option is subject to court approval and to the possible objections of interested parties, possibly including the Department of Public Welfare. Generally, it is preferable to plan *before* any guardianship proceedings are begun and *before* institutionalization.

CHAPTER EIGHT

Avoiding Medicaid Liens

*F*or many years, the states were very lax about enforcing their rights to recover benefits from a Medicaid recipient's estate and placing a lien on his property. Generally, this was because not so many people were entering nursing homes and Medicaid costs were not so great. In view of the fact that annual Medicaid costs now run into the billions, however, this attitude has changed dramatically. Thanks to the 1993 OBRA law, states must now aggressively exercise their rights of recovery against the estates of deceased Medicaid recipients, and again thanks to the OBRA, they may go even further than that.

Lifetime Liens

While federal law allows a lien (a form of attachment) to be placed upon a person's home at the time he becomes a permanent resident of a nursing home, not all states have adopted this law. Even in those states that have, the state may *not* force a sale of the home if a spouse or a child (of any age) or a sibling of the person is living in the home, so long as the child has lived in the home for at least two years prior to the person's institutionalization and cared for the person some or all of that time, and, in the case of a sibling, so long as the sibling lived in the home for at least one year prior to the person's institutionalization. There is no requirement for the sibling to have taken care of the institutionalized person.

Important Note

> Those states that impose a lien on the home (or other real estate) of an institutionalized person after he enters a nursing home could collect before the person's death if the home is sold while the person is alive. If there is a sale during the person's lifetime, however, the state can recover only from the portion of the proceeds attributable to the ownership share of the institutionalized person. For instance, if the institutionalized person was a joint owner with her two children, then the state could only recover from one-third of the sales proceeds. If the property is *not* sold before the person's death, then the state may only recover from the person's probate estate, despite the imposition of the lifetime lien, unless the state has adopted the "expanded" definition of estate, as discussed later.

As noted, the imposition of the lien during lifetime does not, by itself, force a sale. However, there may be circumstances where a "forced" sale could take place. If none of the prescribed relatives or individuals is living in the home and if it is determined that the individual will never be able to return home *AND* if the individual declares (either on his own or through a representative) that he does not intend to return home, then the state can count the home as a resource and terminate benefits. Since in most cases the home is not immediately saleable, the state can agree to continue benefits while the sale efforts take place, if a written agreement to sell is given to the state. In effect, this is a forced sale of the home.

Surprisingly, when the home is sold, it may be, depending upon the practice in the particular state, that the receipt of the proceeds will *prospectively* disqualify the individual and that the proceeds would not have to be used to pay back the state for benefits paid during the "holding period." However, this also varies from state to state, and some states may seek or recover benefits from the time the home became "countable."

Liens at Death

Under Medicaid law, the states have the right to recover Medicaid benefits paid after the benefits recipient dies, but the recovery is limited to assets in the recipient's "estate." For many years, it was clear that the term "estate" meant only the recipient's *probate* estate. The probate estate includes only assets that were in the deceased recipient's *sole* name, so that assets in joint names with another, or in trust, or held under a life estate, for instance, were not part of the probate estate and therefore escaped the Medicaid lien.

Though this is still the law, OBRA 1993 took it one step *further* and gave the states the *option to expand* the definition of estate to include virtually all nonprobate assets, such as jointly held assets, life estates, and trust assets, *"to the extent of"* the recipient's legal interest in such assets at his death. Because it was (at least in the past) so easy to avoid probate and therefore avoid the Medicaid lien, a number of states are not wasting time in adopting laws to expand their definition of estate. (As of June 1994 twelve states had decided to do so and eleven more were considering it.) Given the intent and the trend, it is likely that some form of expanded definition of estate will be with us soon.

This means that the states will be able to go after assets that automatically pass to others (outside probate) at the recipient's death, but in which the recipient had an interest, *to the extent of* that interest. This is where the planning will come in. If the recipient was an equal joint tenant, for example, the state (if it adopts the expanded definition of estate) will be able to reach half the value of the jointly held property. The recovery is in the form of a *sale,* since the asset involved would not be cash but note that in some cases, the state may have to wait before recovery can be realized.

Conditions attached to recovery (there must be no surviving

spouse or dependent child) operate to defer the state's right to collect the funds until some future date. That is, if the deceased Medicaid recipient leaves a spouse, the state may place a lien on the estate property but may *not* collect or enforce the lien until the death of the surviving spouse. Similarly, a lien may attach, but collection cannot be made, while there is a child who is blind, disabled, or under twenty-one who survives the recipient.

To Illustrate

> Jake was seventy-seven when he died and for ten years had been in a nursing home on Medicaid. During that period the state paid him Medicaid benefits of $280,000. Jake owned a home jointly with his wife, Jill, and a life insurance policy that left $90,000 to (ugh!) Jake's probate estate, never a good idea. Jake's home state has adopted a law expanding the definition of estate for Medicaid purposes to include jointly owned property.
>
> On Jake's death, the state may place a lien on the life insurance proceeds (because they became a part of his probate estate) *and* on the home, since it is part of Jake's expanded estate. However, the state may not touch the life insurance proceeds *or* the home, until *after* Jill's death. Jill may not make withdrawals of principal from the insurance account, but she may use the interest. Because of the lien, it is unlikely that Jill will be able to sell or refinance the home, but she can live there. On Jill's death, the state can then take the $90,000 of insurance proceeds, and it can force a sale of the home and apply one-half the proceeds toward the balance of its recovery of the $280,000 in benefits it paid to Jake.

If there had been enough cash in the estate to settle the state's claim, the state would likely have pushed for that. If the family refused, the state might also ask for interest on the debt, although the practice in most states has been to seek recovery of Medicaid benefits paid *without* adding interest.

If, for some reason, Jill was unable or unwilling to settle the state's claim, the state's lien on the home (which would have the same effect as a mortgage) would protect the state's "interest" in the property. As with the life insurance proceeds, the lien would remain on the house until Jill's death, or until the $280,000 was paid or compromised.

As noted, because of the lien, Jill would not be able to sell or refinance the property, although, as noted previously, she would be entitled to live there without interference. When she died, if the heirs still resisted settlement, the state would force a sale of the house, provided that Jake had no surviving child who was blind, disabled, or under twenty-one at the time. The proceeds of the sale would be used to pay the $280,000 owed to the state. Anything remaining would be distributed according to the terms of Jill's will.

If the home was not in joint names and was left to Jill under Jake's will, or if neither Jill nor any of the children occupied the home as a residence, the state usually would attempt to persuade the family to sell or refinance the home and use the proceeds to settle the Medicaid debt. However, the fact that they are not living in the home does *not* give the state any additional rights. The law does not require that the spouse (or dependent children) live in the home or use any of the deceased's probate property in order to prevent the state from forcing a sale of that property to recover Medicaid benefits.

Finally, if there were no surviving spouse and no blind, disabled, or under-twenty-one children who survived the deceased recipient, then the state would *not* have to wait at all. It would have every right to collect against whatever assets were in the estate after all taxes, estate settlement costs, fees, and secured debts were paid. Anything that was left after all of that (probably some old clothes, used furniture, and a broken lawnmower) could finally pass to the family, free and clear.

The expanded definition of estate, although definitely a worry, still offers the opportunity to plan. Remember, federal law only allows the state to recover against the nonprobate assets *"to the extent of"* the deceased recipient's legal interest in the asset, at the moment prior to his death. As explained above, for jointly held assets in which the deceased has an equal interest, this means his equal share of the value of the property at his death. And whatever his share is, with joint ownership the share remains constant from the time of acquisition until his death. However, for life estates or trusts in which he held only an income interest, this means the present value of his life estate or income interest at the moment of his death. This type of interest is *not* constant. It continually *decreases* from the time of acquisition to zero at the time of death. Thus there is an advantage to this form of ownership because the share that may be reachable by the state becomes less and less with the passage of time.

To Illustrate

> Hugh, age seventy-eight, transferred his home to his two children, reserving a life estate. At the time of the transfer Hugh's life estate was worth 47 percent of the value of the home. Ten years later (at age eighty-eight) and after Hugh had been on Medicaid for six years, he died. The state (which had adopted the expanded definition of estate) moved to recover from Hugh's estate. At his death, however, the value of Hugh's life estate (i.e., the "extent of his interest" in the property) was only about 30 percent of the value of the home, and that is all the state can collect.

Tip

> Even with the expanded definition of estate, where nonprobate assets may be subject to recovery, it will be better to avoid probate, because assets that are subject to probate will be *fully* recoverable by the state (up to the amount of benefits paid), whereas recovery against nonprobate assets is limited to the recipient's legal share of those assets.

In summary, any property in the deceased recipient's *probate* estate will be reachable by the state to recover Medicaid benefits as allowed by law. If the deceased recipient has probate assets and leaves a surviving spouse and/or children who are under twenty-one or blind or disabled, the state may file a lien against property in the deceased's probate estate to secure its recovery but will have to wait to actually recover against the property. Property that passes *outside* the recipient's probate estate will generally escape the state's reach, unless the state has adopted the expanded definition of estate. If it has, then it may recover against nonprobate assets, but *only* to the extent of the recipient's legal share of that property. Therefore, it will still make sense to avoid probate.

CHAPTER NINE

Medicaid Appeals

*N*obody is perfect, and that clearly includes the states and their employees. It is quite possible that a Medicaid case worker or other state Medicaid representative will recommend a denial (or termination) of Medicaid benefits or make a determination of a spousal income or resource allowance that appears incorrect and does not meet with the approval of the individual or his family. Fortunately, the law provides for appeal of these determinations, entitling everyone to a "fair hearing" of his case.

Appeal of a Denial of Benefits

If a Medicaid applicant is otherwise eligible to receive Medicaid on account of age or disability, the state will usually deny benefits only if the applicant has too much income or too many assets (as outlined in Chapters 1 and 2) to qualify for Medicaid. The reason for the denial will be stated on the Notice of Denial that is sent to you by the state Department of Public Welfare or other corresponding agency.

If you disagree with the denial and believe that an opportunity to argue and explain your position would result in your qualifying for benefits, you have a right to appeal the denial. To appeal, you (or someone on behalf of the institutionalized person) must sign the request for a fair hearing, *being careful* to respond within the time stated on the notice of denial. This is usually as little as thirty but not more than ninety days from the date of the notice. The notice will tell you.

Tip

It is a good idea to send your request by certified mail, return receipt requested, so that you have proof of the mailing.

If, for some reason, you fail to meet the deadline, you can re-apply for Medicaid. When you receive the next denial, you can file an appeal at that time. The problem with this, however, is the added cost of the nursing home between your two applications. That is, unless you qualify for retroactive benefits, Medicaid, once approved, will pay only for the period beginning with the first day of the month in which you applied for benefits. Therefore, if you miss the first appeal period, you can miss as much as two or three months of benefits.

To Illustrate

Say that on September 10, you apply for Medicaid benefits. On October 8, you are notified that you are not eligible for a reason that you feel you can refute. You file a timely appeal on November 1, and after a hearing, you are granted benefits, which will begin as of September 1, the month in which you originally applied for benefits. If, on the other hand, you *missed* the appeal period, you would then have to re-apply and start over again sometime after November 8 (thirty days from the notice). This would mean that benefits could not begin sooner than November 1, causing you to lose benefits for the months of September and October (unless you qualify for retroactive benefits). In practice, it is likely to be even longer, since some states often take two to three months just to process your application.

Within a short time after your request for a hearing is received by the agency (at least three to four weeks), you will receive notice of the date set for your appeal hearing. If the time and date are not convenient, you can reschedule it by calling the agency, but generally you have the right to only *one* postponement. The hearing will be held in an office of the Hearings Division of the Medicaid agency, although, if you are physically disabled, you may request a hearing at home. (If you do this, you must provide proof of your physical disability.) If the applicant is unable to speak English, the agency is usually required to provide an interpreter.

A "referee" of the Hearings Division will conduct the hearing, and he or she is the one who ultimately renders a decision at this level. The hearing is relatively informal; it is usually held in a conference room with everyone sitting around a table, and each party has the opportunity to freely state his case. In other words, it is *not* held in a courtroom setting and parties are not restricted by any formal rules of evidence. However, the testimony *is* taken under oath and it must be recorded (generally tape recorded), in the event you later decide to appeal the referee's decision to a court.

You may go to the hearing yourself, and you may bring someone with you, such as another member of the family or a friend or, of course, an attorney. If you are not able to attend, the person attending on your behalf and representing you at the hearing must have your *written* authorization to do so. You should probably have your attorney draw up this authorization.

After everyone who is to testify is sworn in by the referee, the case worker (or other state representative) will present the Department's case, stating why benefits were denied or how the spousal resource or income allowance was determined. Then you will have the opportunity to present your argument and evidence.

If your presentation to the referee involves the testimony of others (witnesses), you may bring them with you as well. If you require the testimony of a witness who is reluctant or refused to come to the hearing, you have the right to force him or her to come in by no-tifying the state hearings office that a witness needs to be subpoenaed.

Important Note

> You should prepare *as carefully as possible* for the hearing. That is, after you have learned the exact reason for denial (or the amount of a spousal allowance, if that is the issue), you should gather and review whatever documentation you have to refute the state's position.

To Illustrate

> Say the case worker has denied your application for Medicaid because of the existence of assets in a joint account with a child, which you claimed did not belong to you. To refute this, you must be able to produce evidence as to the origination of the account or the source of the deposits to the account, show-ing that they were attributable to someone other than you (in this case, your child). This could, for instance, consist of deposit receipts that coincided (in time and amount) with bonuses re-ceived from the child's employment, or gifts he or she received from a third party. As a last resort, if you have no other evi-dence, you may submit the child's sworn statement, but this may not be sufficient to convince the referee that the funds belonged to the child.

You also have the right to see and copy whatever informa-tion the case worker has in the file that may be used against you. If you want to review the file, you must contact the case worker to arrange to do so before the scheduled hearing date. In some cases you may need to file a written request.

You should not feel that because the referee is employed by the state welfare agency you will not get a fair hearing. In general, I have found that the referees or hearing officers make every effort to listen to all the facts and (in most cases) make a fair decision. They are not at all hesitant to overturn a case worker's denial of benefits where it is called for. But keep in mind they know the "ropes" as well as they know the law. So if you don't have support for your position, it probably won't be worth your while to request an appeal.

If you lose your appeal but still feel that your argument is worth pursuing, you can appeal the referee's decision, but at this point it can get expensive, because this next appeal must be taken to the appropriate state court, and it would be foolish to do this without an attorney. It is possible to request a rehearing at the same level before *another* referee for "good cause," but this is still an appeal within the state welfare agency and should be considered only when the first referee did not follow the clear dictates of the law or, for some other reason, did not, in your advisor's opinion, conduct a fair hearing.

Important Note _____

> The law requires the state to make a decision on your appeal *within ninety days* of your request for the hearing. You then have only thirty days after the state's decision, if you do not agree with it, to appeal to the appropriate state court. However, if the state fails to notify you of the referee's decision, it may be that your appeal is *"deemed to be denied"* at the end of the ninety-day period. Therefore, if you wait too long for the state to respond, you could *lose* your right to make a further appeal. Therefore, *pay strict attention to the applicable time periods.* In this regard, it is best to check with an attorney to determine the deadlines, as no leeway is given.

Persons already on Medicaid must complete a *Redetermination* form, usually every six months, though federal law suggests no later than every twelve months. This is to allow the agency to determine if the recipient is still eligible to receive benefits. The Redetermination form asks a number of questions about income, assets, and transfers of assets. If, when you file a Redetermination form, your Medicaid benefits are terminated, you have the same rights of appeal outlined above. However, in this case, it may be that your request for a fair hearing must be made within a *much shorter period* (often fifteen days). Appeal within this period may enable you to *continue* to receive Medicaid benefits until a decision is made by the Hearings office. If you do not appeal within the short time period, benefits will be terminated, but you will still have the usual time (from date of denial of benefits) to appeal.

If you subsequently lose your appeal after a continuation of benefits, the agency has the right to *recover* the benefits paid to you during the period that benefits were continued (and possibly the right to recover more, depending on the reason for termination of benefits). As with the appeal of denial of benefits, the referee's decision can be appealed to the appropriate state court.

Appeal to Increase the Spousal Allowance

As discussed in Chapter 2, the state must establish a spousal *resource* allowance at the time an individual is admitted to a nursing home for all Medicaid applicants entering a nursing home on or after September 30, 1989. However, the state will not determine the spousal *income* allowance until the time a person becomes eligible for Medicaid, *unless* the institutionalized spouse or the healthy spouse (or a legal representative of either) requests it earlier.

Tip

> For planning purposes, it is almost always advisable to make this request (for a determination of the income allowance) as early as possible after institutionalization, *whether or not* the individual will be eligible for Medicaid at such time. Then, if the determination of the resource allowance is inadequate to generate enough income (when added to the healthy spouse's other income) to match the spousal income allowance, you may request a fair hearing, under rules similar to those stated above.
>
> At the hearing, which is supposed to take place within thirty days of your request, the healthy spouse will be given the opportunity to show that the income generated by the resources she is allowed to keep, together with her other income, will be less than the amount of income allowed to her by the state. If the referee agrees, he can increase the spouse's resource allowance to an amount sufficient to generate the

necessary income (examples of this are shown in Chapter 4), and the state must then allow the *additional* assets to be transferred to the healthy spouse. However, as discussed in Chapters 3 and 4, many states are attempting to give the at-home spouse the ill spouse's *income* instead of assets, despite federal law to the contrary. If your state is one of these, be prepared to take additional steps if you wish to protect your assets. Nevertheless, in some cases, even this rule can result in the at-home spouse receiving a higher resource allowance on appeal.

To Illustrate _____

> John has entered a nursing home, and based on the total of $80,000 in countable assets available to John and his wife, Mary, Mary is allowed to keep a spousal resource allowance of $40,000. Their money is invested in 4 percent certificates, so that Mary's $40,000 produces $1,600 per year, or $133 per month. Mary's other income consists of a small pension of $267 per month, and John receives Social Security of $825 per month. Upon Mary's request, the state has allowed Mary a spousal income allowance of $1,380 per month. Since Mary would receive only $1,225 per month from all allowable sources of income ($267 pension plus $825 John's Social Security plus $133 interest on her $40,000 = $1,225 per month), Mary could request a fair hearing and ask that her spousal resource allowance be increased so that she can use it to help earn the necessary additional $155 per month allowed her.

In addition to demonstrating that the income allowance cannot be met by the resource allowance, it is also possible to show that the income allowance is simply not enough, due to "exceptional circumstances resulting in significant financial duress." This may be the basis of a request for a fair hearing to first increase the income allowance and, consequently, to then increase the resource allowance in order to generate the additional income.

According to Medicaid regulations, a request for a fair hearing to increase the spousal resource allowance or the spousal income allowance may be made only at the time the application for Medicaid benefits is made. In many instances, family circumstances delay the application for Medicaid benefits for some time after a spouse is institutionalized.

Tip

If you dispute the state's determination of the spousal resource allowance, you can accelerate the scheduling of a hearing by applying for Medicaid benefits *immediately* upon institution-alization (*even though you realize the applicant does not qualify*). This will save you from having to wait for months or years before a final determination of the resource allowance is made.

CHAPTER TEN

Don't Forget to Plan for the Healthy Spouse

So much attention is given to transferring assets and protecting property when the ill spouse enters a nursing home that planning for the healthy spouse is often totally overlooked. I have seen many situations in which assets were transferred to the healthy spouse, who then unexpectedly predeceased the ill spouse, leaving all of her assets to the ill spouse. The effect of this, of course, would be to immediately *disqualify* the ill spouse from Medicaid benefits until virtually all the assets were spent down for nursing home costs, or until some other allowable disposition of the assets could be made. Therefore, *planning for the healthy spouse's estate is as important as planning for Medicaid benefits for the ill spouse.*

Perhaps the first precaution to take is to prepare a durable power of attorney (see discussion in Chapter 6) for the healthy spouse. This will allow for the execution or completion of an estate plan in the event the healthy spouse becomes incompetent.

Next, the will of the healthy spouse should be carefully reviewed. And, because of the strong likelihood that the healthy spouse's existing will leaves her assets to the ill spouse, it should probably be revised. (See Chapter 4 for the option of establishing a "testamentary trust" for the surviving spouse.) In addition, if the ill spouse was named as the executor, a new executor should be named.

Revisions to the will and estate plan of the healthy spouse may take a number of different forms, depending upon (a) the state of her health, (b) whether she wishes to provide for the institutionalized spouse despite the fact that he may be on Medicaid, and (c) whether she wishes to carry out a Medicaid plan for herself.

If her health is not good but it is unlikely she will be institutionalized, then her plan could take the form of outright gifts to other family members (assuming her spouse has already qualified for Medicaid; if he has not, then gifts by the healthy spouse could disqualify the institutionalized spouse as discussed in Chapter 3).

If her health is good, or if it is not good but she is not likely to be institutionalized for the foreseeable future, she may consider a Medicaid plan for herself. The plan could consist of gifts or an irrevocable trust or a combination of both. The trust would have to be an income-only trust as explained in Chapter 4 and would incur a waiting period of up to sixty months (before Medicaid eligibility), depending upon the amount she transfers to the trust.

If she wishes to provide for her husband, it could be done through her Medicaid trust, in which case he could only get the income, and this would not begin until after the death of the healthy spouse. If she wished to provide him more than that, it would have to be done through a "testamentary" trust (under her will), but this would preclude her own Medicaid planning, since it would mean keeping the assets in her own name.

Important Reminder

The Medicaid laws do not count the assets in a trust for an institutionalized person if the trust is funded through the *probate* estate of the person's deceased spouse. Therefore, some advisors suggest that the healthy spouse keep the assets in her own name, providing that on her death those assets will pass through her probate estate into a trust for the benefit of the institutionalized spouse. (This assumes that the healthy spouse stays "healthy" and is never institutionalized.)

There is another concern that may apply where a healthy spouse has assets and dies before the institutionalized spouse. That is the right of the ill spouse to take a share of the other spouse's estate on her death, regardless of the provisions of the will. This is known as a spouse's "forced share," or "elective share," and every state gives a surviving spouse this right in some form.

The concern is that even though a spouse may have "disinherited" her ill spouse (for Medicaid planning purposes), the state could require the ill spouse to exercise his right to take a share of the other spouse's estate, or that it would at least treat that right as an available asset, thereby disqualifying the spouse from receiving Medicaid benefits. The various states' treatment of this has not been consistent, but it appears that as a matter of practice, if not as a matter of law, they are not forcing the spouse to take the share and are not treating the right to such a share as an asset. Perhaps this is because the right is an elective one that requires positive action to exercise, as opposed to a disclaimer (refusal) of an inheritance, which requires positive action *not* to inherit it. (A *disclaimer* of an inheritance is definitely a problem for Medicaid purposes, because it is generally treated as a disqualifying transfer of a countable asset.)

In summary, planning for the healthy spouse should go hand in hand with planning for the ill or institutionalized spouse. Otherwise, all gains made in planning for the institutionalized spouse could be lost.

Some Case Studies

$\mathcal{T}$he following case studies are based either on actual cases or on a combination of facts from actual cases. You should not assume, however, that just because your circumstances appear to be similar or even identical to those illustrated, you should take the same action as the family in the case study. Every family is different and there is no substitute or shortcut for the advice of competent counsel who has firsthand knowledge of the family, its circumstances, and its objectives, as well as the applicable federal and local law. Nevertheless, these studies should help you understand the practical application of some of the principles discussed in this book and how they may help the average family faced with long term care.

It should also be noted that the discussions in the following case studies contain only general suggestions about possible transfers of assets or other planning ideas. They do not list or extend to the details of all of the particular documents and steps that might be involved. For instance, although not specifically recommended in the individual case studies, *every* case would warrant the use of a durable power of attorney, as well as a review of any existing wills or trusts. Also, in each of the case studies, it can be assumed that the husband and wife are over sixty-five years of age, unless otherwise noted. Finally, it is important to note that the suggestions made in the various case studies may *not* be the only options available to the family.

CASE 1

Donald and his wife, Edna, have a home worth about $260,000 with a $48,000 mortgage, and a second home on Cape Cod, in Edna's name, worth about $170,000. The family consists of Donald, Edna, and their three adult children. In addition, they have about $55,000 in jointly held savings, to which they contributed equally. Donald is ill and is likely to enter a nursing home within the next several months.

Solution. The couple should use $48,000 of their savings to pay off the mortgage on the home. They should then attempt to rent the summer home (it *could* be rented to the children for a fair rental). This would leave the couple with their home, the summer home, and about $7,000 in savings. Although the summer home is a countable asset, it is likely that the couple would be allowed to keep it as part of Edna's spousal resource allowance because it is producing *income* for the spouse, unless Edna has some other substantial source of income. That is, if the second home is producing a fair market rental of $1,000 per month and Edna's income allowance is $1,000 (or more) per month, she can support the position that the entire home should be attributed to her spousal resource allowance.

Result. The couple's savings, their home, and their summer home are preserved.

CASE 2

Henry and Alice live in the first-floor apartment of their jointly owned three-family home. Their son, Bill, and his wife have rented the second apartment for several years, and the third apartment is also rented. Henry and Alice have savings of $25,000 and live off their Social Security income plus the rents from their home. Henry has been ill for a few years, but his condition has worsened and it appears he will be entering a nursing home within the next several months.

Solution. Henry and Alice should consider deeding their home to Bill, reserving a life estate for Alice only. (There would be little advantage to reserving a life estate for Henry as well, unless they planned to sell the home after Henry's death; see discussion of the tax consequences of life estates in Chapter 4.)

The Medicaid laws permit a transfer of the home to Bill (provided he has lived there for at least two years *and* has provided care for his father for some time during that period that kept Henry from being institutionalized sooner) *without* affecting Henry's eligibility for Medicaid. Alice's retention of a life estate would cause at least half the property to receive a step-up in basis on her death (to reduce subsequent capital gains tax if Bill later sells the home). In the meantime, the income from the rented apartments would be allocated to Alice under the spousal income allowance. (Note that most state laws are unclear as to whether a transfer of a two- or three-family residence in which the applicant resides is clearly considered his *residence*. Technically, only the portion he occupies is his "residence." However, up to now the states have generally treated the entire property as the residence in such cases. Obviously, the greater the number of apartments, the less likely it is that this policy would be applied.)

As to the $25,000 in savings, most if not all of this is likely to be allocated to Alice as a spousal resource allowance. If there is a concern that it may not be allowed in full, Alice could use a portion of these funds to make repairs to the home prior to Henry's admission to a nursing home, or she could give a portion of the funds to Bill under the "half-a-loaf" plan (see Chapters 3 and 4).

Result. The couple's home and savings are totally preserved.

CASE 3

Harry and his wife, Sally, have a condo in Florida, jointly owned and valued at $200,000, and they rent an apartment in Vermont. Their other assets are nominal. They live on pensions received by each of them. Although they maintain a residence in Florida, their roots and their children are in Vermont. Harry is ill and is slated to enter a nursing home in Vermont before the year's end.

Note: If Harry enters a nursing home in Vermont, he cannot at the same time be considered a Florida resident. The value of the condo in Florida would be fully countable for Vermont Medicaid purposes. If Harry and Sally have definitely decided not to place Harry in a Florida nursing home, the condo presents a bit of a problem, but not an insurmountable one.

Solution. It is quite possible for Harry and Sally to have different domiciles, so that Harry could have a Vermont residence and Sally a Florida residence, and both would be exempt. It is also permissible for Harry to make transfers to Sally without jeopardizing his Medicaid eligibility, so long as Sally does not, within the succeeding thirty-six-month period, subsequently transfer those assets to another person. Therefore, Harry can deed over his half of the Florida condo to Sally.

In the subsequent determination of her spousal resource allowance, Sally would claim an *exemption* for the Florida condo as it is *her* residence (assuming she continues to maintain a Florida domicile), and, therefore, Harry should immediately qualify for Medicaid. At some future date, Sally can plan for the disposition of the Florida condo, either through a trust or through a deed to the children with a reserved life estate, *without* affecting Harry's Medicaid eligibility.

Result. The couple has preserved the Florida condo, even though it is situated out-of-state.

As an *alternate* plan, Harry and Sally could sell the Florida property and use the proceeds to purchase their apartment (or another condo) in Vermont, in *Sally's* name. This would be exempt and Harry would immediately qualify for Medicaid.

CASE 4

Jack and his wife, Mabel, have recently sold their jointly owned home and now rent an apartment for $1,000 per month. They live off the income from the $250,000 proceeds of the sale and have no other assets and only nominal income. Jack is ill and about to enter a nursing home.

Solution. First, they should investigate the possibility of purchasing the apartment they live in. If they could purchase it for, say, $150,000, this would immediately protect that amount of funds for Mabel. The balance of $100,000 is very likely to be allowed to her in full (perhaps after a hearing) as her spousal resource allowance, since it is her primary source of income.

If they cannot purchase the apartment, they should consider approaching the landlord to arrange a *prepayment of rent* under their *nonassignable lease.* This may be attractive to the landlord and they may even be able to get a long-term discount on the rent payments. For example, if they prepaid ten years' rent for $100,000, the payment is a permissible transfer for Medicaid purposes (since they received something of equal value for their money), and the couple would be assured of no rental increase for that period. They would record their ten-year prepaid lease with the appropriate registry of deeds, so that they would be protected in the event the property was sold or the owner went bankrupt. Further, if they both died within the ten-year period, their children could either use or rent the apartment for the balance of the prepaid term. The bulk of the remaining funds (though probably not all) could be kept by Mabel as spousal resource allowance. To the extent the state did not allow her to keep all the funds, she could use them (or such amount as she wished) to purchase an annuity for herself.

Result. Most if not all of the couple's savings have been preserved.

CASE 5

John, a widower, lives alone in his $400,000 home, on a pension and Social Security totaling $1,500 per month. His other assets total about $65,000. He and his wife worked all their lives to stay in the home and pay off the mortgage, and now John's hope, like that of most American parents, is to be able to leave his home to his two children. John is quite ill, however, and may not be able to remain in his home much longer.

Solution. John should consider deeding the home to his children, while reserving the right to live there for the rest of his life (a life estate). Since this transfer does *not* fall under one of the exceptions to the transfer rule, the children, and John, must be prepared to cover John's nursing home costs for the thirty-six-month period after the transfer. (His pension and other assets would appear to cover a substantial portion of the costs, and to the extent they do not, it would be worthwhile for the children to use all or part of the $65,000 to pay the difference to protect the home.) After that, John may apply for Medicaid.

On John's death, the home will avoid probate, but the reservation of a life estate will cause the home to be included in John's taxable estate, and his estate may have to pay a state estate tax on it, *if* his state has an estate tax (only six states have a separate estate tax). The return benefit, however, is that the children will receive a step-up in cost basis in the home equal to the value of the home used for estate tax purposes (*whether or not* an estate tax is paid—see discussion of this in Chapter 4). Therefore, a subsequent sale of the home by the children will produce little or no capital gains tax.

As to John's remaining cash savings (if any), after setting aside an amount to cover projected nursing home costs for the thirty-six-month period, the children should apply whatever amount is reasonable to maintain the home and to purchase a pre-paid burial contract or other exempt assets as appropriate. If there are still countable assets left, a portion could be given away as explained in Chapter 3.

Result. The home (and possibly some savings) is preserved and a substantial tax benefit is realized as well.

CASE 6

Bill and his sister, Bertha, live in the home they inherited from their parents several years ago. In addition, they have about $150,000 of jointly held assets. Although Bertha is in good health, Bill has a chronic illness and may have to enter a nursing home within the year.

Solution. Bill can deed his share of the home directly to

Bertha *without* affecting his eligibility for Medicaid, since a transfer of the home to a sibling who has an equity interest in the home (and who has lived in the home for a year or more) is one of the exceptions to the triggering of the thirty-six-month waiting period. However, this does not help protect the remaining assets. Therefore, *before* Bill transfers the home, Bertha should segregate *her* share of the jointly held savings and place them in a separate account. Next (again, *before* the transfer), Bill could use some or all of the balance of *his* savings to make any necessary improvements on his home. Whatever was left, after any other allowable expenses, such as the purchase of a prepaid burial contract and/or home furnishings, would have to be used toward Bill's nursing home care.

Result. The home is preserved for Bill's sister, and possibly a major portion of his savings as well.

CASE 7

John has been in a nursing home for about three months. He and his wife, Mary, have a home (jointly owned and in need of repairs) and about $150,000 in a joint savings account. When John entered the nursing home, Mary was given a spousal resource allowance of $75,000, which means that she must spend $75,000 on John's care before he can qualify for Medicaid.

Solution. Mary places her $75,000 spousal resource allowance in a *separate* account for her own benefit. After determining that the repairs to their home will cost $35,000, she then uses that amount of *John's* funds to make these repairs. This leaves John with $35,000 and Mary with no "countable" funds. Mary then purchases an annuity to provide her with additional income, using *John's* $35,000. Now she applies for Medicaid.

Although Mary's spousal resource allowance has been established, it should follow that after legitimate expenditures, such as making improvements to the family home and the purchase of the annuity, Mary could nevertheless apply for Medicaid for John. Since her own resources are protected as part of the spousal resource allowance, and since John has made no transfers that violate the thirty-six-month rule, he should *immediately* qualify for Medicaid.

Result. Even *after* entrance to a nursing home, the couple's home *and* some savings can still be protected.

Note _____

> Don't forget the estate planning considerations that should accompany such a plan. In this case, for example, I would not leave the $75,000 in Mary's name alone. After John qualifies for Medicaid, I would at least place it in joint names with a child or, *preferably*, in a revocable trust for Mary's benefit, providing that on Mary's death, the balance would pass to the children. Similarly, the home may also be kept in such a trust. (Though, *remember* that when the home is placed in the trust it *loses* its exemption; therefore a revocable trust will be of *no help* if Mary is institutionalized.) They should also each have durable powers of attorney. Finally, I would make sure that Mary's will does not leave her estate to John.

CASE 8

Phillip and his wife, Phyllis, have a home, about $30,000 in a joint savings account, and a small sailboat worth about $12,000. The only other substantial asset is an IRA (Individual Retirement Account) belonging to Phyllis and containing about $110,000. This account was funded with a "rollover" from Phyllis's employer's retirement plan when Phyllis retired. Phillip is seventy and Phyllis is sixty-nine. Phillip is suffering from a chronic illness and is likely to be institutionalized within the next several months.

Though they realize that their home will be protected, as well as the boat in most states (because it is tangible personal property), they are concerned over the assets in Phyllis's IRA. The law allows the state to count the value of this account *in full*, less penalties for early withdrawal. And since Phyllis is over fifty-nine and a half, there will be no such penalties.

Solution. Before Phillip enters a nursing home, Phyllis should direct the custodian of her IRA to purchase an *irrevocable annuity* for her. This is a contract issued by an insurance company that will pay Phyllis a fixed annual amount for her lifetime. Once the contract is purchased, it cannot be "cashed in" or transferred to someone else and, therefore, would have no countable value as an asset for Medicaid purposes. Instead, the annuity payments would be counted as *income,* but the income from the annuity will belong solely to Phyllis and need not be used toward Phillip's care (although it would reduce Phyllis's monthly income allowance granted under the Medicaid laws). The net effect is that their countable assets are now reduced from $140,000 to $30,000, most, if not all, of which will be allowed to Phyllis under the resource allowance, and the balance can easily be protected from countability (for example, by purchase of a burial contract, home improvements, and so on). Phyllis's purchase of the annuity is *not* a disqualifying transfer because she received something of equal value (the income for her lifetime) in return for the money.

Result. The couple has preserved their savings as well as the entire amount of Phyllis's retirement funds.

Tip

> Be sure the annuity is irrevocable and nontransferable, and if it has a "term certain," the term should not exceed Phyllis's life expectancy; otherwise the state may try to count it as an asset rather than income. (See discussion on annuities in Chapter 4.)

Important Note

> Whenever applying the tactic used in the above case study, it is strongly recommended that you consider purchasing an annuity with a "term certain" (that is, one that would guarantee payments for a specified term, such as ten years or fifteen years, to a named beneficiary if the healthy spouse died within the term). This would ensure the receipt of benefits to the family if the healthy spouse met an early death, but if she outlives the term certain, payments will continue for her lifetime. Furthermore, use of the annuity to convert countable assets to income is not necessarily restricted to retirement plan funds. If the circumstances are suitable, an annuity can be used with other funds as well, as illustrated in the next case study.

Another Important Note _____

When purchasing an annuity with a term certain *be careful* that the length of the term certain *does not exceed* the life expectancy of the "annuitant" (generally the person who is purchasing the annuity). If it does, you will have a *disqualifying transfer* of the amount attributable to the period in excess of the life expectancy.

To Illustrate _____

Louise, a widow, age eighty-one, recently entered a nursing home. Louise's only asset is a bank account containing $50,000. To help protect what is left of her life's savings and perhaps leave a little for her daughter, Lilly, Louise uses $48,000 to purchase an annuity with a fifteen-year term certain. If Louise dies within that period, Lilly will continue to receive the payments for the balance of the term.

However, because Louise's life expectancy (approximately six and a half years according to federal tables) is far less than the fifteen-year term certain, Louise's purchase of the annuity will be treated as a *disqualifying transfer* to the extent of the value of the amount of the guaranteed payments that will be paid to her daughter beyond Louise's life expectancy. (Whether she actually ends up living for the fifteen years, or even longer, is irrelevant at the time of the purchase.)

For instance, if $48,000 would buy Louise an annuity of $580 per month for nine years but only $430 per month for fifteen years, the difference (in present value) between the two amounts for the period beyond Louise's life expectancy (i.e., fifteen years less six and a half years) will constitute a *gift* (and therefore a disqualifying transfer for Medicaid purposes) to Louise's daughter *at the time of the purchase.* Of course, all the payments that Louise does receive will have to be applied toward her care in any event.

Note _____

For inexplicable reasons, some insurance companies are reluctant to issue term-certain annuities to persons of "advanced age" (generally those who may pass age eighty-five during the term certain). If you have this problem, you may instead consider a policy with an "installment refund option." This is an arrangement that at least guarantees that you (or your beneficiary) will get your investment back if you die too soon.

Warning

The purchase of an annuity, whether commercial or private, to convert assets to income is a tactic that some states are trying to attack, largely because it works so well in special situations and is *clearly allowable under the law.* Therefore, be prepared for an attempt to change the law to close this loophole.

CASE 9

Brenda, age fifty-nine, and her husband, Eddie, age sixty-six, rent an apartment in Manhattan and have a home on Cape Cod that they have used during the summers. The jointly owned Cape Cod home is worth about $225,000 (no mortgage), and they have about $160,000 in joint savings, mostly from Eddie's earnings. Eddie is suffering from an illness that is likely to lead to his institutionalization in the near future. Brenda has been advised that if she does nothing, she will lose the Cape home plus all but about $75,000 of their savings.

Solution. Brenda and Eddie (or even Brenda, alone) can move into the Cape Cod home and immediately treat it as their principal residence. This will render the full value of that residence exempt and, therefore, noncountable as an asset for Medicaid purposes. Next, and before Eddie enters the nursing home, Brenda should take a major portion of their savings, say $125,000, and purchase an annuity contract that will pay her a fixed monthly income for the rest of her life. For instance, at her age, for $125,000 Brenda could purchase an annuity that would pay her about $950 per month for her life with a fifteen-year term certain. This means that if she died within the first fifteen years, the $950 per month would be paid for the balance of the fifteen-year period to a beneficiary Brenda would name when she purchased the annuity (for example, her children). (If Brenda were concerned about providing for her husband, she could purchase a "joint and survivor" annuity, which would pay a little less per month, but would continue payments for *both* their lives and could *still* contain the fifteen-year term-certain option. In fact, if it is a joint and survivor annuity, the term certain could be *extended* to cover their *combined* life expectancy.)

The effect of the purchase of the annuity would be to convert the fully countable savings into *noncountable income* for Brenda. That is, although the income to Brenda would count against her $1,500 maximum monthly income allowance,* the $125,000 used to purchase the annuity would no longer be a countable asset. The thirty-six-month waiting period will not apply to the purchase of the annuity because it is a transfer for full consideration (she got something of equal value in return).

Brenda would *also* be entitled to one-half the remaining $45,000 savings as her spousal resource allowance (or, in some states, all of it, since it is less than the allowable maximum of $74,820) and the balance of the savings could easily be used to improve their home, purchase an automobile, and so on.

Result. They have saved their home and most or all of their savings, while insuring Brenda an income for life.

Note

Alternatively, and perhaps providing an even *better* result, Brenda could wait until *after* Eddie entered a nursing home (after the determination of her spousal resource allowance) to make the purchase of the annuity, which could actually leave her with even *more* cash.

To Illustrate

When Eddie is institutionalized, Brenda will be allowed about $75,000 as her spousal resource allowance, leaving a balance of $85,000 in their savings account. After Brenda segregates *her* $75,000, she could use $85,000 of Eddie's money to purchase an annuity as discussed. This is entirely permissible for the reasons stated in the case solution and would leave Brenda

* Adjusted each year for inflation: 1995 = $1,870 per month

with $75,000 available cash instead of $22,000, as in the first illustration.

Conclusion

As cautioned at the outset of this book as well as at the outset of this chapter, there can be no single reference source that will give you the perfect Medicaid planning formula for every family situation. While these illustrations, explanations, and case studies offer many ideas, some of which should prove extremely helpful to you, there is no way to anticipate the peculiarities or special circumstances in every case, or the particular regulations in each state. Furthermore, the Medicaid laws and regulations have gone through a number of changes over the past few years, and, undoubtedly, there will be more.

Therefore, as with an estate plan, a Medicaid plan should be reviewed *at least* every year to see if it is still the best plan in light of the present state of the law. Those who created irrevocable Medicaid trusts prior to the 1986 COBRA change (discussed in Chapter 4) know exactly what I mean. This is also a good illustration of how the government views Medicaid planning techniques—the more popular and successful certain techniques become in protecting the assets of middle-class families, the more likely that the government will change the law to attack those techniques.

Many do not think this is fair, particularly those in the "middle class," who are too rich to be on welfare but too poor to afford the skyrocketing costs of long term nursing home care. Is it fair that a cancer patient will have all of his costs of care covered, while an Alzheimer's patient or one with multiple sclerosis must be driven into poverty? What is the rationale behind the government's covering catastrophic medical problems while ignoring catastrophic custodial care problems? Both are beyond the control of the patient! Something is clearly wrong with this, and perhaps our government will soon recognize the paradox.

In the meantime, you must, if you want to protect your assets and your family's security, make sure you are aware of the planning options available to you and seek the necessary expert advice in carrying out what appears to be the best plan for you. As to what is the "best" plan, only time will tell, but you can definitely increase the odds in your favor by getting a second expert opinion on any plan that is recommended to you. It will be well worth the time and the expense, and you can think of it as part of the cost of your "health care insurance."

States That Place a Limit on Income for Medicaid Purposes

$\mathcal{T}$he following states are referred to as "income cap" states, as they have laws that restrict Medicaid eligibility to those persons who have income *below* a specified amount.

If a person who is domiciled in one of these states has income (from *any* source) that exceeds the allowable limit, *by even one dollar,* he will *not* be able to receive Medicaid benefits (even though he qualifies in every other respect) until his income drops to (or below) the allowable limit.

Alabama	Idaho	South Carolina
Alaska	Iowa	South Dakota
Arkansas	Louisiana*	Tennessee
Colorado	Nevada	Texas
Delaware	New Jersey	Wyoming
Florida	New Mexico	
Georgia	Oklahoma	

* As of July 1, 1992, the cap applies only to noninstitutionalized individuals.

The monthly income limits in these states have ranged from $854 to $1,221 per month in the recent past. Because these limits change from time to time, it is best to check the current income limit in your state by calling the local Medicaid office (see Appendix C). The 1995 amount was $1,374.

Summary of State Gift Tax Laws

Only six states (Connecticut, Delaware, Louisiana, New York, North Carolina, and Tennessee) still had a gift tax as of January 1, 1995. Their provisions are briefly summarized below. Be aware, however, that these laws contain many more details and exceptions. Before you make any gifts, you should check your local tax expert.

Connecticut
Taxable gift rates range from 1% for gifts up to $25,000 to 6% for gifts in excess of $200,000. The tax does not apply to property situated outside Connecticut. Otherwise, no "tax-free" gifts.

Delaware
Taxable gift is the amount subject to the federal gift tax in each calendar year and is basically computed in the same way, except that the federal unified credit is not allowed. The rates range from 1% for

the first $25,000 of taxable gifts to 6% of the taxable gifts in excess of $200,000.

Louisiana
Donor has a $30,000 specific lifetime exemption plus a $10,000 annual exclusion per donee. Rates: 2% for the first $15,000 of gifts over annual exclusion plus lifetime exemption; 3% for gifts over $15,000. Gifts to spouses are exempt.

New York
Gift tax ranges from 3% for taxable gifts over $50,000 to 21% for taxable gifts in excess of $10.1 million. Gifts to spouses are not subject to gift tax. There is a unified credit allowed to offset the gift tax. Credit is $2,950 but is reduced to $500 where the computed gift tax is $5,400 or more.

North Carolina
The gift taxes are imposed at different rates depending on the class of the donee. Class A donees: lineal issue, lineal ancestor, husband, wife, stepchild, adopted child. Class B donees: brother, sister, descendant of either, or aunt, or uncle (by blood). Class C: all others except gifts to charitable purposes. Donor has $100,000 specific lifetime exemption for taxable gifts to Class A donee plus $10,000 annual exclusion per donee for all classes including Class A. Gifts to a spouse are tax-free.

Rates: Class A: 1% to 12% (for taxable gifts over $3 million)
        Class B: 4% to 16% (for taxable gifts over $3 million)
        Class C: 1% to 17% (for taxable gifts over $2.5 million)

Tennessee
Gift tax rates depend on the class of the donee. Class A donees: husband, wife, lineal ancestor or descendant, brother, sister, stepchild, son or daughter-in-law, and adopted child. Class B: all others except charities, nonprofit institutions, etc. Marital deduction: one-half of the gift to the spouse. Annual exclusion for Class A gifts is $10,000

and for Class B gifts, $3,000. There is also a single exemption for each calendar year of $10,000 for Class A gifts and $5,000 for Class B gifts.

Rates: Class A: 5.5% to 9.5% (for taxable gifts over $440,000)
               Class B: 6.5% to 15% (for taxable gifts over $200,000)

State Medicaid Offices

$\mathcal{T}$he following are the addresses and telephone numbers of the Medicaid offices in the various states. A great deal of information can be learned by simply calling and asking for an "application package" for Medicaid benefits. The package will include the necessary forms, a brief explanation of the Medicaid programs, and (in some states) eligibility requirements. In addition, the package should include instructions for completing the application, indicating what assets and transfers of assets must be shown on the application.

Alabama
Alabama Medicaid Agency
2500 Fairlane Drive
Montgomery, AL 36130
(205) 277-2710

Alaska
Division of Medical Assistance
Dept. of Health & Social
Services

P.O. Box H
Juneau, AK 99811
(907) 465-3355

Arizona
Arizona Health Care Cost
Containment System (AHCCS)
801 East Jefferson
Phoenix, AZ 85034
(602) 244-3655

Arkansas
Arkansas Dept. of Human
Resources
Medicaid
P.O. Box 1437
Little Rock, AR 72203
(501) 682-8502

California
Medical Care Services
Dept. of Health Services
714 P Street, Room 1253
Sacramento, CA 95814
(916) 332-5824

Colorado
Colorado Dept. of Social Services
Health & Medical Services
1575 Sherman Street, 10th Floor
Denver, CO 80203
(303) 866-5901

Connecticut
Dept. of Income Maintenance
110 Bartholomew Avenue
Hartford, CT 06106
(203) 566-2008

Delaware
Division of Social Services
Dept. of Health & Social Services
Medicaid
P.O. Box 906
1901 N. Dupont Highway
Briggs Building
New Castle, DE 19720
(302) 421-6140

District of Columbia
Office of Health Care Financing
DC Dept. of Human Services
2100 Martin Luther King, Jr.
Avenue SE
Suite 302
Washington, DC 20020
(202) 727-0735

Florida
Medicaid Provider/Consumer
Relations
1317 Winewood Boulevard
Building 6, Room 260
Tallahassee, FL 32399
(904) 488-8291

Georgia
Georgia Dept. of Medical
Assistance
2 Martin Luther King, Jr. Drive
1220-C West Tower
Atlanta, GA 30334
(404) 656-4479

Hawaii
Health Care Administration
Dept. of Human Services
P.O. Box 339
Honolulu, HI 96809
(808) 586-5392

Idaho
Bureau of Welfare Medical
Programs
Dept. of Health & Welfare
405 W. State Street
Boise, ID 83720
(208) 334-5747

Illinois
Division of Medical Programs
Illinois Dept. of Public Aid
201 S. Grand Avenue East

Springfield, IL 62743
(217) 782-2570

Indiana
Indiana State Dept. of Public
Welfare
100 N. Senate Avenue
State Office Building, Rm 701
Indianapolis, IN 46204
(317) 232-6865

Iowa
Division of Medical Services
Dept. of Human Services
Hoover State Office Building
Des Moines, IA 50319
(515) 281-8621

Kansas
Dept. of Social &
Rehabilitative Services
Division of Medical Services
1915 Harrison Street
Docking State Office
Building
Room 628-S
Topeka, KS 66612
(913) 296-3981

Kentucky
Dept. of Medicaid Services
275 E. Main Street, 3rd Floor
Frankfort, KY 40621
(502) 564-4321

Louisiana
Bureau of Health Services
Financing
P.O. Box 91031
Baton Rouge, LA 70821
(504) 342-3956

Maine
Dept. of Human Services
Bureau of Income Maintenance
State House, Station #11
Whitten Road
Augusta, ME 04333
(207) 289-5088

Maryland
Medical Care Policy
Administration
201 W. Preston Street
Baltimore, MD 21201
(301) 225-1432

Massachusetts
Division of Medical Assistance
650 Washington Street
Boston, MA 02111
(617) 348-5500

Michigan
Medical Services Administration
Dept. of Social Services
P.O. Box 30037
Lansing, MI 48909
(517) 335-5000

Minnesota
Dept. of Human Services
Health Care Programs Division
444 Lafayette Road
St. Paul, MN 55155
(612) 296-8517

Mississippi
Division of Medicaid
801 Robert E. Lee Building
239 N. Lamar Street
Jackson, MS 39201
(601) 359-6050

Missouri
Division of Medical Services
Dept. of Social Services
P.O. Box 6500
Jefferson City, MO 65102
(314) 751-3425

Montana
Medicaid Services Division
Dept. of Social &
Rehabilitation Services
111 Sanders Street
P.O. Box 4210
Helena, MT 59604
(406) 444-4540

Nebraska
Nebraska Dept. of Social Services
301 Centennial Mall South
P.O. Box 95026
Lincoln, NE 68509
(402) 471-3121

Nevada
Division of Welfare
Dept. of Human Resources
2527 N. Carson Street
Carson City, NV 89710
(702) 687-4378

New Hampshire
Division of Human Services
Office of Medical Services
6 Hazen Drive
Concord, NH 03301
(603) 271-4344

New Jersey
Division of Medical Assistance
& Health Services
Dept. of Human Services
CN-712

7 Quakerbridge Plaza
Trenton, NJ 08625
(609) 588-2600

New Mexico
Medical Assistance Division
Dept. of Human Services
P.O. Box 2348
Santa Fe, NM 87504
(505) 827-4315

New York
Division of Medical Assistance
New York State Dept. of Social
Services
40 N. Pearl Street
Albany, NY 12243
(518) 474-9132

North Carolina
Division of Medical Assistance
Dept. of Human Resources
1985 Umstead Drive
P.O. Box 29529
Raleigh, NC 27626
(919) 733-2060

North Dakota
North Dakota Dept. of Human
Services
Medical Services
600 East Boulevard
Bismarck, ND 58505
(701) 224-2321

Ohio
Dept. of Human Services
Medicaid Administration
30 E. Broad Street, 31st Floor
Columbus, OH 43266
(614) 644-0140

Oklahoma

Division of Medical Services
Dept. of Human Services
P.O. Box 25352
Oklahoma City, OK 73125
(405) 557-2539

Oregon

Office of Medical Assistance
Dept. of Human Resources
203 Public Service
Building
Salem, OR 97310
(503) 378-2263

Pennsylvania

Dept. of Public Welfare
Health & Welfare Building
P.O. Box 2675
Harrisburg, PA 17120
(717) 787-3119

Puerto Rico

Dept. of Social Services
P.O. Box 11398
Santurce, PR 00910
(809) 722-7400

Rhode Island

Dept. of Human Services
600 New London Avenue
Cranston, RI 02920
(401) 464-3575

South Carolina

South Carolina Health &
Human Services Finance
Commission
1801 Main Street
Columbia, SC 29201
(803) 253-6128

South Dakota

Medical Services
Dept. of Social Services
700 Governor's Drive
Kneip Building
Pierre, SD 57501
(605) 773-3495

Tennessee

Bureau of Medicaid
729 Church Street
Nashville, TN 37247
(615) 741-0213

Texas

Dept. of Human Services
Health Care Services
P.O. Box 149030
Austin, TX 78714
(512) 450-3050

Utah

Division of Health Care Financing
Utah Dept. of Health
P.O. Box 16580
Salt Lake City, UT 84116
(801) 538-6151

Vermont

Dept. of Social Welfare
Vermont Agency of Human Services
103 S. Main Street
Waterbury, VT 05676
(802) 241-2880

Virginia

Virginia Dept. of Medical
Assistance Services
600 E. Broad Street, Suite 1300
Richmond, VA 23212
(804) 786-7933

Washington

Medicaid Recipient
Assistance & Information
617 8th Avenue SE
Olympia, WA 98504
1-800-562-3022

West Virginia

Division of Medical Care
West Virginia Dept. of Human
Services
State Capital Complex
Building 6, Room 717B
Charleston, WV 25305
(304) 348-8990

Wisconsin

Division of Health
Wisconsin Dept. of Health &
Social Services
P.O. Box 309
Madison, WI 53701
(608) 266-2522

Wyoming

Medical Assistance Services
Dept. of Health & Social Services
6101 Yellowstone
Cheyenne, WY 82002
(307) 777-7531

APPENDIX D _____

State Agencies on Aging

*T*hese agencies provide information on sources of assistance for older Americans, free of charge.

Alabama
Commission on Aging
Montgomery, AL 36130
Toll free (within state)
1-800-243-5463
(205) 242-5743

Alaska
Older Alaskans Commission
P.O. Box C, MS 0209
Juneau, AK 99811
(907) 465-3250

Arizona
Department of Economic Security
Aging and Adult Administration
1400 W. Washington Street

Phoenix, AZ 85007
(602) 542-4446

Arkansas
Division of Aging and Adult Services
Donaghey Plaza South
Suite 1417
7th and Main Streets
P.O. Box 1417/Slot 1412
Little Rock, AR 72203-1437
(501) 682-2441

California
Department of Aging
1600 K Street
Sacramento, CA 95814
(916) 322-3887

Colorado
Aging and Adult Services
Department of Social Services
1575 Sherman St., 10th Floor
Denver, CO 80203-1714
(303) 866-3851

Connecticut
Department of Aging
175 Main Street
Hartford, CT 06106
Toll free (within state)
1-800-443-9946
(203) 566-7772

Delaware
Division of Aging
Department of Health and Social
Services
1901 N. Dupont Highway
New Castle, DE 19720
(302) 421-6791

District of Columbia
Office on Aging
1424 K Street, N.W., 2nd Floor
Washington, DC 20005
(202) 724-5626
(202) 724-5622

Florida
Office of Aging and Adult Services
1317 Winewood Boulevard
Tallahassee, FL 32301
(904) 488-8922

Georgia
Office of Aging
Department of Human Resources
878 Peachtree Street NE, Room 632
Atlanta, GA 30309
(404) 894-5333

Hawaii
Executive Office on Aging
335 Merchant Street
Room 241
Honolulu, HI 96813
(808) 586-0100

Idaho
Office on Aging
Statehouse, Room 108
Boise, ID 83720
(208) 334-3833

Illinois
Department of Aging
421 E. Capitol Avenue
Springfield, IL 62701
(217) 785-2870

Indiana
Department of Human
Services
251 North Illinois Street
P.O. Box 7083
Indianapolis, IN 46207-7083
(317) 232-7020

Iowa
Department of Elder Affairs
Jewett Building, Suite 236
914 Grand Avenue
Des Moines, IA 50319
(515) 281-5187

Kansas
Department of Aging
122-S Docking State Office
Building
915 SW Harrison
Topeka, KS 66612-1500
(913) 296-4986

Kentucky

Division for Aging Services
Department for Social Services
275 E. Main Street
Frankfort, KY 40621
(502) 564-6930

Louisiana

Governor's Office of Elderly
Affairs
P.O. Box 80374
Baton Rouge, LA 70898-0374
(504) 925-1700

Maine

Bureau of Elder & Adult Services
State House, Station 11
Augusta, ME 04333
(207) 624-5335

Maryland

State Agency on Aging
301 W. Preston Street
Room 1004
Baltimore, MD 21201
(301) 225-1102

Massachusetts

Executive Office of Elder Affairs
38 Chauncy Street
Boston, MA 02111
Toll free (within state)
1-800-882-2003
(617) 727-7750

Michigan

Office of Services to the Aging
P.O. Box 30026
Lansing, MI 48909
(517) 373-8230

Minnesota

Minnesota Board on Aging
Human Services Building
4th Floor
444 Lafayette Road
St. Paul, MN 55155-3843
(612) 296-2770

Mississippi

Council on Aging
421 W. Pascagoula Street
Jackson, MS 39203-3524
Toll free (within state)
1-800-222-7622
(601) 949-2070

Missouri

Division of Aging
Department of Social Services
P.O. Box 1337-615
Howerton Court
Jefferson, MO 65102-1337
(314) 751-3082

Montana

The Governor's Office on Aging
State Capital Building
Room 219
Helena, MT 59620
Toll free (within state)
1-800-332-2272
(406) 444-3111

Nebraska

Department on Aging
State Office Building
301 Centennial Mall
South
Lincoln, NE 68509
(402) 471-2306

Nevada

Department of Human Resources
Division for Aging Services
340 No. 11th Street, Suite 114
Las Vegas, NV 89101
(702) 687-4210

New Hampshire

Department of Health and Human
Services
Division of Elderly and Adult
Services
6 Hazen Drive
Concord, NH 03301
(603) 271-4680

New Jersey

Department of Community Affairs
Division on Aging
S. Broad and Front Sts., CN 807
Trenton, NJ 08625-0807
Toll free (within state)
1-800-792-8820
(609) 292-0920

New Mexico

Agency on Aging
La Villa Rivera Bldg., 4th Floor
224 E. Palace Avenue
Santa Fe, NM 87501
Toll free (within state)
1-800-432-2080
(505) 827-7640

New York

State Office for the Aging
2 Empire State Plaza
Albany, NY 12223-0001
Toll free (within state)
1-800-342-9871
(518) 474-5731

North Carolina

Department of Human Resources
Division of Aging
693 Palmer Drive
Raleigh, NC 27626-0531
(919) 733-3983

North Dakota

Department of Human Services
Aging Services Division
State Capitol Building
Bismarck, ND 58505
(701) 224-2577

Ohio

Department of Aging
50 W. Broad Street
8th Floor
Columbus, OH 43266-0501
(614) 466-1221

Oklahoma

Department of Human Services
Aging Services Division
P.O. Box 25352
Oklahoma City, OK 73125
(405) 521-2327

Oregon

Department of Human Resources
Senior Services Division
313 Public Service Building
Salem, OR 97310
Toll free (within state)
1-800-232-3020
(503) 378-4728

Pennsylvania

Department of Aging
231 State Street

Barto Building
Harrisburg, PA 17101
(717) 783-1550

Rhode Island
Department of Elderly Affairs
160 Pine Street
Providence, RI 02903
(401) 277-2858

South Carolina
Commission on Aging
400 Arbor Lake Drive
Suite B-500
Columbia, SC 29223
(803) 735-0210

South Dakota
Agency on Aging
Adult Services and Aging
Richard F. Kneip Building
700 Governor's Drive
Pierre, SD 57501-2291
(605) 773-3656

Tennessee
Commission on Aging
706 Church Street, Suite 201
Nashville, TN 37219-5573
(615) 741-2056

Texas
Department on Aging
P.O. Box 12786
Capitol Station
Austin, TX 78741-3702
(512) 444-2727

Utah
Division of Aging and Adult Services
120 North 200 West

P.O. Box 45500
Salt Lake City, UT 84145-0500
(801) 538-3910

Vermont
Office on Aging
Waterbury Complex
103 S. Main Street
Waterbury, VT 05676
(802) 241-2400

Virginia
Department for the Aging
700 Centre, 10th Floor
700 E. Franklin Street
Richmond, VA 23219-2327
Toll free (within state)
1-800-552-4464
(804) 225-2271

Virgin Islands
Department of Human Services
19 Estate Diamond
Frederick Sted
St. Croix, VI 00840
(809) 772-4850

Washington
Aging & Adult Services
Administration
Department of Social and Health
Services
Mail Stop OB-44-A
Olympia, WA 98504
(206) 586-3768

West Virginia
Commission on Aging
State Capitol Complex
Holly Grove
Charleston, WV 25305

Toll free (within state)
1-800-642-3671
(304) 348-3317

Wisconsin
Bureau on Aging
Department of Health and Social
Services
P.O. Box 7851
Madison, WI 53707
Toll free (within state)

1-800-242-1060
(608) 266-2536

Wyoming
Commission on Aging
Hathaway Building
First Floor
Cheyenne, WY 82002
Toll free (within state)
1-800-442-2766
(307) 777-7986

Index

Attorney-in-fact, 114, 121
Automobiles, 17–18, 37

Bank accounts, joint, 11, 20–21,
   59, 113
Beneficiaries
   disclaimer of inheritance, 42, 148
   life insurance, 16, 17
   trusts, 72, 85
Blindness, eligibility rules, 8. *See
   also* Disabled child
Burial accounts, segregated, 15
Burial contracts, prepaid, 15–16
Burial plots, 15

California, 25, 117, 120
Capital gains taxes, 61, 62, 64, 65,
   69, 93
Catastrophic illness, Medicaid/
   Medicare coverage for, 3–5
"Categorical" eligibility, 7, 8. *See
   also* Age; Disability
Children. *See also* Disabled child
   gifting principal residence to,
      61–63
   guardianship and Medicaid plan-
      ning for, 127
   payment for services rendered,
      51, 54–56
   reimbursements to, 56–58
   selling principal residence to, 61
COBRA (Consolidated Omnibus
   Reconciliation Act), 74, 75
Colorado, 127, 163
Commercial annuities, 53
Compensation
   attorney-in-fact, 121
   children/relatives, 51, 54, 56–
      58
Connecticut, 119, 121, 127, 165

Conservators, 27, 114, 118,
   125–127. *See also* Guardians
Consolidated Omnibus Reconciliation Act (COBRA), 74, 75
Convertible trusts, 82–83
Countable assets
   changing to exempt, 50–51
   changing to income, 51–54
   defined, 12
   gifts of, disqualification period
      and, 44–45
   married persons, 24
   out-of-state home as, 70–71
"Cure" for a disqualifying transfer,
   37, 41–42, 48–49
Custodial care, 6, 107

Delaware, 163, 165–166
Disability, eligibility rules, 8,
   39–40, 77–78
Disabled child
   Medicaid liens and, 134–136
   transfers of assets to, 36, 39, 45
Disclaimer of inheritance, 42–43,
   148
Disqualification period. *See* Waiting
   period
Disqualifying transfer of assets,
   "cure" for, 37, 41–42, 48–49
Divorce/separation, 98–99, 101, 102
Durable power of attorney
   advantages of, 115–116
   defined, 114
   for health care decisions,
      122–123
   healthy spouse, planning for,
      146
   incompetent persons, 125
   overview, 112–113
   states' special rules, 121–122
   third parties and, 120